start
beading

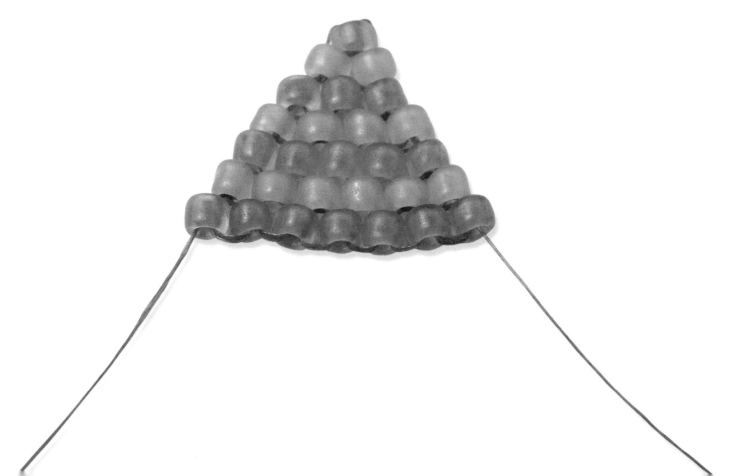

start
beading

All you need to know to create
beautiful beaded accessories

Stephanie Burnham

APPLE

A QUARTO BOOK

First published in the UK in 2006 by
Apple Press
Sheridan House
114 Western Road
Hove BN3 1DD
United Kingdom
www.apple-press.com

ISBN-10: 1-84543-137-5
ISBN-13: 978-1-84543-137-2

QUAR.BEAB

Conceived, designed and produced by
Quarto Publishing plc
The Old Brewery
6 Blundell Street
London N7 9BH

Editor: Michelle Pickering
Art editor: Julie Joubinaux
Designer: Jon Wainwright
Photographer: Phil Wilkins
Illustrator: Kate Simunek
Indexer: Dorothy Frame
Assistant art director: Penny Cobb

Art director: Moira Clinch
Publisher: Paul Carslake

Colour separation by Provision Pte Ltd, Singapore
Printed by Star Standard Industries Pte Ltd, Singapore

9 8 7 6 5 4 3 2 1

CONTENTS

INTRODUCTION

The purpose of this book is both to instruct and to inspire you to create your own beaded jewellery and accessories. Complete beginners who have not previously picked up a bead or beading needle will find projects that are easy to work and stylish to wear. More experienced beaders will find ideas that will encourage them to take their work in new directions.

The book starts with an overview of the tools and materials you will need. You will be happy to discover that a beading needle, some beading thread and a selection of beads are enough to get going, so even a complete novice can give beadwork a try without having to purchase lots of expensive items. Supplies of beads, tools, findings, wires and threads are readily available from bead stores, mail-order services, and online bead suppliers (you will find a list of resources on page 124). This chapter also provides some guidance on how to mix and match colours to create pleasing results.

Then comes the heart of the book: the techniques and projects. This chapter has been organized so that you learn the different techniques of beadwork progressively. The first few pages of each section are devoted to a particular beadwork technique, explaining the basic technique and providing useful variations. These pages are followed by two or more projects that use the basic technique you have just learned. What better or more rewarding way to master the technique than to practise it by making beautiful beaded jewellery.

Both the techniques and the projects are written clearly and concisely, with enlarged step-by-step photographs that are easy to comprehend and that will quickly inspire confidence. Some steps also have close-up 'satellite' photos, so you can see a particular step through from beginning to end. There are also a few techniques that are used in most beadwork pieces, such as starting and finishing off threads, plus ideas for embellishments to give your pieces that final touch.

From learning about what materials to work with and how to attach clasps to threading a bead loom and adding a fringe, this book will give you a superb grounding in the craft of beadwork. Once you have discovered how fantastic working with beads can be, you will soon have the confidence to adapt and experiment with the techniques to create stunning pieces of beadwork that are uniquely your own.

TOOLS AND MATERIALS

When you first become interested in working with beads and start to look around in speciality bead stores and on the Internet, it soon becomes apparent that there is a huge range of tools and materials available. Buying at this stage without knowing exactly what you need can be costly and result in your buying items unnecessarily. Start by looking through the projects in this book and decide which you would like to tackle first. Then you can arm yourself with a small shopping list before you make any purchases. Start with a small selection and build up your collection gradually. As far as beads are concerned, a good rule of thumb is to buy what appeals to you – you can be sure that at some point you will incorporate them into your designs.

Another important thing to consider when starting beadwork is where you are going to work. Good lighting is essential because some beads are very small. You may even need a magnifying glass to ensure that you do not strain your eyes. A good chair is also important, as well as a work surface that is at the correct height so that you do not lean over and strain your back. Getting your working environment right will make your beading all the more enjoyable.

BEADS

Beads are available in such a huge range of shapes, sizes, colours and designs that the choice can seem overwhelming at first. When purchasing beads, buy the best quality you can afford. Try to avoid cheap beads because they may be misshapen or break easily, so you could end up discarding more than you use. They may also have sharp, uneven edges that can cause the beading thread to break and so ruin a piece of beadwork.

SEED BEADS

The term seed bead refers to any small bead. Usually made of glass, the most common type is round, but triangle, cube and cylinder seed beads are also popular and widely available. They work well in most beadweaving techniques, and are also used as decorative spacers between accent beads. Whenever the generic term *seed bead* is used, both throughout this book and in beadwork in general, it is the round seed beads that are being referred to. Seed beads are produced in Japan, the Czech Republic, India, China and France, and are commonly sold by gram weight.

◀▶ **Round beads**
Usually referred to simply as seed beads, these small round beads are also known as rocaille. They are available in a variety of sizes, including 6, 8, 11 and 15mm, and in many different colours and finishes. Their round, polished shape means that these beads blend and mold together well, making them ideal for all beadweaving techniques.

BEADER'S TIP

Even if a pattern or book project states how many seed beads are required, always buy more than specified. You may have to discard some beads as you work, perhaps because they are sharp-edged or misshapen, or you may break or lose some. Beads are made and dyed in batches, so if you have to buy more beads to finish a piece, you may well find that the new beads vary in colour from those in the rest of the project. It may also take some time before your bead supplier has more supplies, or a colour may occasionally be discontinued.

◀▼ **Bugle beads**
These long, cylindrical tubes are available in several sizes, including 4 and 6mm. Most seed beads are 'tumbled' in the factory to smooth the edges, but bugles are not because they would break. They start life as long tubes of glass that are cut to the correct lengths. This means that they can have sharp edges, so always check bugles before incorporating them into your design. Discard any sharp-edged beads because they will cut the beading thread and ruin your beadwork. Cheaper bugles, in particular, tend to be quite badly cut, but even the best-quality Japanese bugles need to be checked carefully before use.

◄► Triangle beads

Triangle beads are available in a variety of sizes, including 5, 8 and 10mm, and in a wide range of colours and finishes. Although the beads are triangular, the hole through the centre is usually round. Triangle beads mold together very well, almost like the scales of an animal, and give added shape and texture to a design.

▼► Japanese cylinder beads

Often referred to by their brand names – Miyuki Delicas, Toho Treasures and Toho Aiko – these small cylindrical beads have an extra-large hole through the centre. They are extremely high in quality, and are among the most regular, uniform beads available in the world today. These beads mold together beautifully, making them ideal for pictorial or patterned beadwork.

◄► Cube beads

Cube beads are square, usually with a round hole through the centre. The most commonly used and widely available size is 4mm. They are available in a wide variety of colours, and help to give strength and stability to a design.

THE CUFF OF THIS CHARM BRACELET (PROJECT 11) IS MADE FROM ROUND SEED BEADS INTERSPERSED WITH CUBE BEADS, WHILE TWO STYLES OF FLOWER ACCENT BEADS FORM THE CHARMS.

ACCENT BEADS

Along with seed beads, the projects in this book also feature accent beads. This term is used to refer to any beads that stand out from the seed beads as a special feature of the design. These include faceted crystals, drop beads, shells, flowers, stars and charms, and are made of a variety of materials, from glass to metal. Glass accent beads are available in the greatest variety of shapes, colours and sizes, and come from many different countries around the world, including India, China, Italy and the Czech Republic. There is also a multitude of plastic beads, from inexpensive, brightly coloured children's beads to collectable plastics such as Bakelite. Other materials used to make beads include metal, wood, shell, ceramic and semiprecious stones.

◀ **Glass-blown beads**
These glass beads are handblown individually, often with surface decoration added afterwards. They tend to be more expensive because the beads are made one at a time.

▼ **Austrian crystal beads**
The famous Swarovski company in Austria has been producing these popular crystal beads for many years.

▶ **Dichroic beads**
Dichroic glass is especially made for glass artists producing their own glass beads.

◀ **Czech Republic beads**
These accent beads are made from special pattern molds passed down through generations of families.

▼ ▶ Plastic beads

There are plenty of inexpensive, cheerful plastic beads available, and good-quality plastic beads can easily be mistaken for glass ones. It is not until you pick one up and feel the lightness of it that you realize it is made from plastic.

▼ Metallized plastic beads

These plastic beads are covered in a very durable plastic coating in different metallic finishes.

▼ ▶ Metal beads

Metal beads are available in highly prized metals such as gold and silver as well as base metals such as copper, brass and aluminium. They are produced around the world, including Thailand, India and Bali. Many countries also make ranges of plated metal beads.

▼ Shell and pearl beads

Whole or sliced shells and pearls, available with pre-drilled holes, can be threaded into many beadwork designs. Their iridescence is perfect for making eye-catching pieces of jewellery.

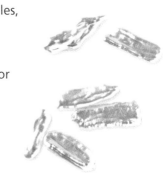

Tools

Many of the tools used for beadworking can be bought from your local hardware store, craft store or, if you are lucky enough to have one nearby, bead supplier. Also check the Internet and the resources on page 124. For many of the beadwork techniques featured in this book, the only essential tools are a needle and scissors. Purchase additional equipment, such as pliers for wirework, as you progress.

▲ Beading mat

A beading mat is not essential, but it does make working with beads easier. The mat is made of a soft, foamlike material so that the beads sit right on top of it but will not roll around, making them easy to pick up with a needle without the needle getting caught in any pile. It also allows you to have all the beads you are using out at once instead of having to keep opening and closing bead containers.

◄ Beading needles

Beading needles are available in both long and short lengths. Long needles are easier for beginners to work with for most beadwork techniques, but short needles (sometimes called sharps) are easier for netting stitch.

Needles are also available in different thicknesses. The size you use will be determined by the size of the beads, the type of thread and the stitch being used. As a general guide, size 10 needles are suitable for most beadwork projects, while size 13 needles are great for loomwork and square stitch, when a slightly finer needle is required.

▼ Beading loom

Looms are available in several forms, from inexpensive plastic versions to expandable looms made from the best-quality wood. It is a good idea to start with an inexpensive loom to see if you enjoy this type of beadwork. If you do, you can invest in a more expensive good-quality loom later. Looms are available from most craft and bead stores, but you could always improvise and build your own using a wooden rectangle and nails.

► Scissors

A small, sharp pair of scissors is essential for cutting thread ends cleanly and evenly.

◄ Round nose pliers

These pliers have smooth, round 'noses' that are used to shape wire into loops and rings. A pair with neat, short noses is best because they will allow you to make small, neat loops and maintain good control of the work.

► Chain nose pliers

These pliers have pointed noses that are round on the outside and flat on the inside. They are used for opening and closing small chain links, as well as for tucking in ends of wire in tight places.

▲ Flat nose pliers

These pliers have flat ends that are useful for holding wire and bending it at angles. They can hold several strands of wire securely and are also useful for closing jump rings.

▲ Cutting pliers

These do what their name says: they cut wire. If you are using memory wire, you will need heavy-duty cutters or special memory wire cutters.

◄ Flush cutters

These allow you to cut wire absolutely flush to your work. They have small, neat, pointed ends that will go into small spaces.

THREADS

Beads can be threaded onto many different materials, from synthetic and natural threads to wire and cord. The one you choose will often depend on personal preference, but you will certainly need to consider the weight of the beads and the size of their holes. Always choose the strongest thread possible, but remain aware that you want movement and flexibility in your designs. Nymo, a brand of nylon beading thread, has been used for most of the work in this book because it is strong and durable, but some beadworkers prefer to use polyester or linen thread. If you get the chance to try out different threads, work a small test piece – you may come across a technique that requires a different thread treatment.

▲ Thread conditioner

Some beading threads are already waxed, or you can apply a synthetic thread conditioner or beeswax to your beading thread to help stop it from splitting. Simply hold the thread underneath your thumb on top of the conditioner, then pull the thread through. The thread is now evenly coated and ready to start beading.

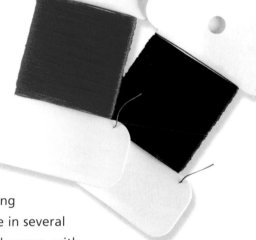

▲ ▶ Synthetic beading threads

Available in a variety of colours and several thicknesses, synthetic threads are good all-round beading threads. Nymo thread is a fine nylon filament, available in several thicknesses. Polyester thread is available in greater thicknesses, with thicker threads often being waxed to aid threading. Synthetic thread is very strong, but it does stretch slightly over time.

▶ Natural threads

Both silk and linen threads are available in many wonderful colours and thicknesses, but they are not quite as strong as synthetic threads. Leather thonging and cords such as rat's tail are also available in different colours and thicknesses. The beads are usually strung directly onto the cord without the use of a needle.

▼ Beading wire and tiger tail

Beading wire and tiger tail are composed of multiple strands of very fine steel cables held together in a plastic or nylon coating. Available in a variety of thicknesses or gauges, they are both great for stringing beads and can be used without needles – the beads are simply threaded straight onto the wire. Tiger tail is the less expensive option, but it does kink quite easily.

Memory wire

This is a strong, pre-coiled wire made in different diameters that is suitable for chokers, bracelets and rings. The beads are simply threaded directly onto the wire, which is why it is included here in the thread section.

▶ Elastic

Fine, medium and thick beading elastic is available from bead suppliers. It can also be bought from craft and sewing stores.

FINDINGS

Strictly speaking, the term *findings* refers to all the components used to make a piece of jewellery. However, most people use it to refer to the mechanical parts that are used to assemble the jewellery – for example, earring wires and clasps. These findings are often decorative as well as functional. Using the right findings for the piece you are making is very important, because it can mean the difference between a beautifully finished item and a spoiled one.

METALWORK FINDINGS

This first section describes findings that consist of the bits and pieces of metalwork used within the bead or wirework design; the second section on page 20 deals with the various clasps and fastenings available. Most findings are available in plated or pure metals, in silver or gold colours. It is advisable to use sterling silver or gold for earwires.

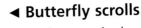

◄ Ear posts and ear wires

Ear posts are straight pieces of wire that fit directly into a pierced ear. Ear wires are a shepherd's crook shape that slides through the hole in the ear. Both types are available with a small loop at the front to which you can attach the main body of the earring.

◄ Butterfly scrolls

These fit onto the back of ear posts to hold the earrings securely in place.

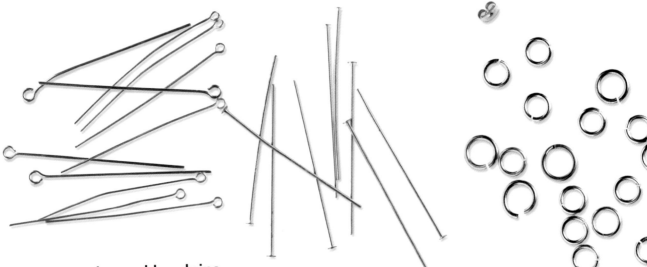

▲ Eyepins and headpins

These are used as a support for beads when creating earrings. Headpins are also used to attach beads and charms to a chain bracelet. Headpins look like small nails, with the flat head of the pin preventing the beads from falling off. Eyepins have a small loop of wire at the head of the pin, from which you can dangle a drop bead.

▲ Jump rings

These circles of metal are used either for linking pieces together or for attaching a fastener. They are easy to open and close using pliers.

▶ Split rings

These are double circles of metal that work just like the rings on the end of a keychain. They have the same uses as jump rings but are more secure.

▶ Flat leather crimps

Leather crimps are used to attach fasteners to cotton, leather, suede or ribbon by clamping the thonging between the crimps. The fastener is then attached to the loop at the end of the crimp for a truly professional finish.

◀ Calottes and knot cups

These consist of two half spheres with a small loop at one end. The spheres are closed around the knot at the end of a string of beads and a fastener is attached to the loop. Calottes, also known as clam shells, cover the knot sideways; knot cups, also known as bead tips, have a hole between the two half spheres through which the thread passes before it is tied into a knot.

▲ Cones and end caps

These are widely used to finish multi-strand necklaces and bracelets. End caps come in a variety of shapes; cones are, obviously, conical.

◀ End bars

These are used to finish a multi-row necklace or bracelet, with a fastening attached to the other side.

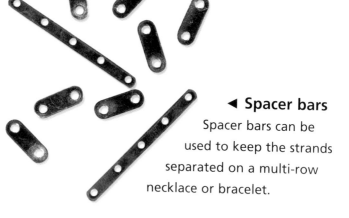

◀ Spacer bars

Spacer bars can be used to keep the strands separated on a multi-row necklace or bracelet.

FASTENINGS AND CLASPS

There are numerous different types of fastenings and clasps available, in many shapes, sizes and finishes. Remember that a good closure can really complement your design. Many people skimp on clasps, preferring a less expensive one that seems like a bargain, but unfortunately this often shows. Think of all the expense, time and effort that went into creating your finished piece – isn't it worth finishing off well with a great clasp?

▶ Lobster clasps

Lobster clasps are discrete and tidy, and probably the most useful fastener to have in your stash. The lobster clasp is fitted to one end of the finished piece, with a jump ring or split ring opposite to fasten it to. These clasps look great on bracelets and necklaces, but if using the smaller sizes, they can be a little awkward to fasten on your own.

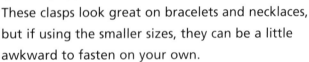

◀ Magnetic clasps

Magnetic clasps are great for anyone with dexterity problems, because they often have quite strong magnets and stick together really well. They are available in many finishes, from sterling silver and gold to nickel-free plated. The problem with them is that they love to attach themselves to steel objects without your knowing. They are also unsuitable for people with pacemakers.

◀ Toggle clasps

A toggle clasp consists of a ring and a T-bar section, each with a looped fixing point for attaching the clasp to the finished item. Toggle clasps work well on necklaces and bracelets, and are quite easy to fasten. They are available in many sizes, from tiny to fairly large, but be careful not to use too big a toggle or it will detract from the design. Place the toggle alongside the piece first to check that it looks good.

▲ Bar clasps

These come in two-, three-, four- and five-bar sizes. They are a great help when creating cuff bracelets because, with several fixing points along the clasp for extra security, they hold the entire width of the bracelet in place.

◄ Simple clasps

These clasps, including spring rings, box clasps, barrel clasps and fish hook clasps, tend to be at the less expensive end of the market and usually have only one small fixing point at each side of the clasp. They are not always a good fit and can be very stiff for the first few uses. They are certainly not very easy to open for anyone with arthritis because they require a lot of pressure. However, if you are making jewellery for a bazaar or charity and you need to keep costs down, they will certainly help.

▲ Hook and loop fasteners

The hook is attached to one side of the piece, with the loop on the other side. This type of fastener is easy to open and close but not as secure as some other clasp styles.

► Elaborate clasps

These clasps speak for themselves. They are nicely finished, with really good colour and design. They would finish off any design perfectly and are well worth the initial outlay.

▲ Clamping clasps

This clasp has a large staplelike fastener at each end, together with a lobster clasp and chain extension for securing. The clasp is designed to clamp down onto the ends of wire knitting or ribbon, using flat nose pliers to secure it.

▼ Sieve brooches and brooch backs

Sieve brooches have two pieces: a mesh section and a brooch back. The mesh section can be decorated with beads and wire, then clamped onto the brooch back. Brooch backs can be sewn onto the back of a finished design that you wish to make into a brooch.

COLOUR THEORY

One of the most exciting features of beadworking is the impact of colour, but many people who are new to the craft say that they find colour really challenging, and there are so many beads to choose from that they feel overwhelmed. Some people seem to have more of an aptitude for colour than others, but it is possible to learn how to use it to great effect by exploring the basic principles of colour theory. Always remember, however, that colour is a personal choice and that there are no hard-and-fast rules.

THE COLOUR WHEEL

The relationship between different colours can be demonstrated on a colour wheel showing the primary, secondary and tertiary colours. The primary colours are red, yellow and blue. The secondary colours sit between pairs of primaries and are made by mixing those two primary colours together. The secondary colours are orange (a mixture of yellow and red), green (a mixture of yellow and blue) and violet

(a mixture of blue and red). The tertiary colours sit between each pair of primary and secondary colours because they are produced by mixing those two colours together, making red-orange, yellow-orange, yellow-green, blue-green, blue-violet and red-violet. Lighter tints can be created by adding white to each colour. Darker shades can be created by adding black to each colour.

COLOUR QUALITIES

Colours that are opposite on the colour wheel are called complementary, or contrasting; for example, blue and orange. They create vibrancy when placed next to each other. Colours that sit next to each other on the colour wheel are called analogous, or harmonious; for example, yellow, yellow-orange and orange. They produce a more subtle and harmonious effect when used together, because they each contain some of the same colour.

Red

Red-orange

Red-violet

Orange

Violet

Yellow-orange

Blue-violet

Yellow

Blue

Yellow-green

Blue-green

Green

NEUTRALS

Neutral colours, such as white, black, cream, brown and grey, do not appear as pure colours on the colour wheel but are made by mixing pure colours together. For example, if an artist mixed pigments of all three primaries together in equal intensities, the result would be black. Mixing pigments of colours opposite each other on the colour wheel produces a range of greys and browns. Neutrals, therefore, work well with all colours on the colour wheel and can be used to great effect in beadwork, especially in backgrounds and to set off other colours.

VALUE AND TEMPERATURE

Other characteristics to keep in mind when choosing colours are whether their tonal value is light or dark and whether they are warm or cool colours. Reds and browns are generally warm colours, whereas blues and greens are cool. In general, warm colours tend to advance and cool colours tend to recede. The same is true with dark and light tones of the same colour – dark tones tend to advance and light tones tend to recede.

TERMINOLOGY

Hue: This is the actual colour on the wheel: red, blue and green, for example.

Tint: Any hue with the addition of white to make the colour paler.

Shade: This is the hue with the addition of black, or any other dark colour to make it darker.

Tonal value: All tints and shades are tones of a colour in relation to black or white. Tonal value describes the lightness or darkness of a colour on a scale from white to black.

THIS BRACELET (PROJECT 5) IS MADE FROM SEED BEADS IN A SPECTRUM OF 12 COLOURS. USE THE COLOUR WHEEL TO HELP YOU SELECT YOUR PALETTE OF RAINBOW COLOURS.

COLOUR SCHEMES

When planning a project, it is a good idea to get out your bead tubes and experiment with putting different colours together. Many people choose colours based on a gut feeling, but it is often helpful to refer to a colour wheel (page 22). Spend time sorting through your bead colours. By placing them on the wheel, you will soon see schemes coming together. You could always take a colour wheel with you when purchasing beads. It will help you and ultimately stop you from making mistakes when selecting colours for a project.

ANALOGOUS SCHEME

These are colours, including tints and shades, that lie next to each other on the wheel. You can choose from two to six colours – a third of the complete colour wheel. Be aware that if you choose an analogous colour scheme and your beads are similar in tonal value, your project will look lovely but may lack impact. Adding a small amount of a complementary colour to analogous colours – a touch of orange to blues and violets, for example – will provide sparkle.

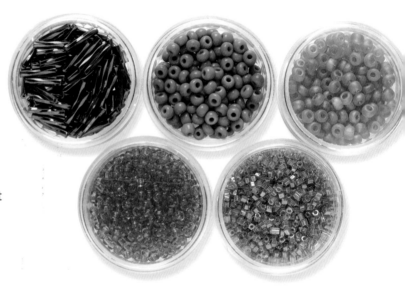

COMPLEMENTARY SCHEME

Choosing colours that are opposite each other on the wheel will produce the greatest amount of contrast. Complementary colours may clash with each other when used at full strength, so try tints and shades. Alternatively, follow the 80:20 rule – that is, 80 per cent of one colour and 20 per cent of the complementary colour. If you use 50 per cent of each colour, they can fight and the result will not be as restful to look at.

MONOCHROMATIC SCHEME

Single-colour, monochromatic schemes can work very well if you include beads of different shades and tints of the main colour.

SAMPLE SCHEMES

Examine the colour schemes used in the projects to see how different colours work together. You might like to try experimenting with your own beads to come up with alternative colour schemes.

Project 1: Seashore bracelet

The shell embellishment was the starting point for this colour scheme. There are browns, greens and peaches within the shells, so a warm brown for the seed bead base is an appropriate choice. Green, peach and matt brown are used in the branch fringing to give added texture and depth to the piece.

Project 17: Wirework charm bracelet

The gold chain works harmoniously with the different tones of green beads, while splashes of orange give the bracelet impact. However, if you choose a silver chain, you could try adding pinks, purples or even a touch of black or crystal to produce a dramatic effect.

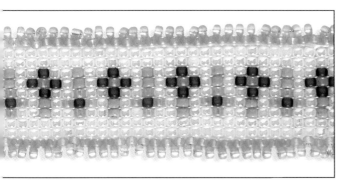

Project 12: Friendship bracelet

This design could be worked in almost any colour scheme. Pearlized cream seed beads give the bracelet a fresh summer look, but you could choose to work the background in a much darker colour to give a more dramatic impact to the design.

Project 14: Meteor shower bracelet

This monochromatic piece has a distinctly evening feel, with crystal beads down the spine to add sparkle and shine. The project could be given a very different look by using spring/summer colours for the base, with the addition of flower and leaf accent beads on the spine.

TECHNIQUES AND PROJECTS

This book has been created primarily for anyone who has ever thought about trying jewellery making but never had the confidence or found detailed enough instructions to make attempting it possible. Each of the techniques featured in the book has been split into small, easy-to-follow sections so that the technical step-by-step method of how to work the stitches is featured first, followed directly by two or more projects employing that particular technique. So, if you do get stuck, you only need to flip back one or two pages to remind yourself how to work a particular stitch.

Although this book explains beadwork right from the basics, the projects range from simple to more elaborate designs that will appeal to experienced beaders as well as to beginners. Even if you are already familiar with a technique, you may find some of the tips and step-by-step explanations useful. This chapter provides a taste of most of the main beadwork techniques and will hopefully inspire you to go on expanding your skills and discovering this wonderful and relaxing craft.

Technique: PEYOTE STITCH

Peyote stitch is one of the most versatile off-loom techniques, producing a flexible piece of beadwork that feels almost like fabric. The tension of the thread plays a major part in the appearance and texture of the stitch. A stop bead is used to prevent beads from falling off the tail end of the thread, as well as to tighten the tension of the beadwork. Peyote is best worked with a single strand of thread, but use two strands to create a firmer base for freestanding and three-dimensional beadwork.

EVEN-COUNT PEYOTE

For beginners, peyote stitch is easier to achieve with an even number of beads. An odd count involves manoeuvring the needle and thread through several beads to arrive in the right place and direction to start the next row, so it should only be attempted once you have mastered working with an even count.

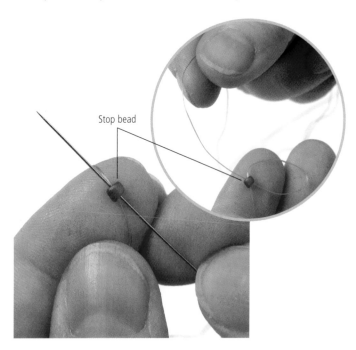

Stop bead

step 1 Thread a beading needle with 1m (1yd) of beading thread. Slide a bead to within 15cm (6in) of the tail end of the thread. Bring the needle back up through the bead to create a loop around the bead. This is called the stop bead.

Getting the tension right

The first two or three rows of peyote stitch can be difficult to control because the beads move about a lot, so it is best to hold the rows between a thumb and forefinger rather than trying to bead on a table. To tighten the tension, pull the working end of the thread firmly in the direction you are beading. When the row is complete, use a thumbnail to push the stop bead towards the main beadwork.

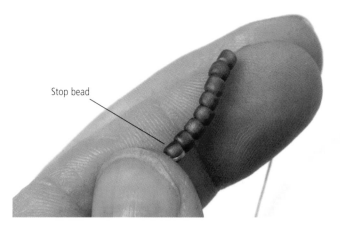

Stop bead

step 2 Thread on seven more beads, pulling the thread through so that all eight beads sit snugly together.

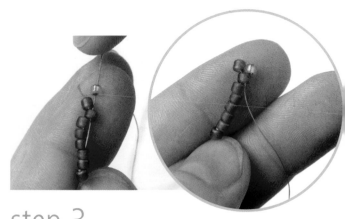

step 3 Holding all the threaded beads between a thumb and forefinger, pick up another bead with the needle, then take the needle through the next to last bead on the first row.

4 beads
on row 2

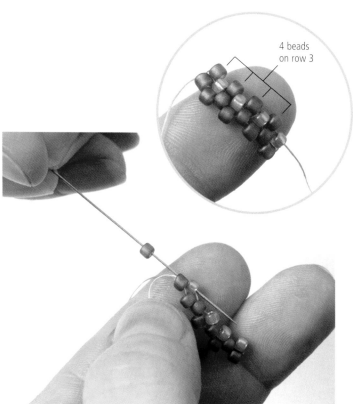

4 beads
on row 3

step 4 Continue along the row, taking the needle through every other bead, until you have added four beads. Two colours of beads are used here to make the different rows easy to see. Note the gaps between the beads on row 2. This is where you need to place the beads for the next row.

step 5 Pick up another bead with the needle to start row 3. Take the needle through the last bead added on row 2, which should be sitting slightly raised above the first row of beads. Continue in this way to the end of the row. You should have added four beads on row 3.

step 6 At this point, starting row 4, you may find it easier to flip the beadwork over as shown. Continue adding rows of beads until you are confident about working the stitch.

TWO-NEEDLE START

If you find starting peyote stitch a little difficult, you may find it easier to start with two needles instead of one.

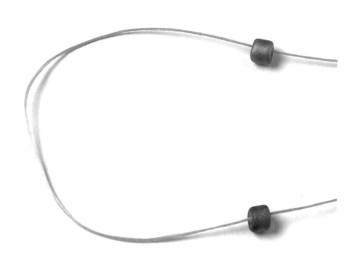

step 1 Thread a beading needle onto each end of a 1m (1yd) length of beading thread. Pick up two beads, taking them down towards the middle of the looped thread.

step 2 Thread a third bead onto one of the needles, then pass the other needle through the same bead. Push the bead down towards the first two beads so that they sit one above the other, with the third bead sitting alongside both.

step 3 Pick up one bead with each needle and push them down towards the first three. Continue in this way until you have the required length of base. When you start the next row, revert to one needle and thread (see Even-count peyote, page 28). Leave the second thread to one side until your working thread runs out.

TUBULAR PEYOTE

Tubular peyote creates a hollow tube of beads and can be worked around any cylindrical object, such as a drinking straw, a piece of dowelling, or a bottle. Beginners may find it helpful to use a cylinder made of transparent material so that the work can be seen clearly. If you start with an even number of beads, as demonstrated here, you will need to step up at the end of each row in order to move the needle up to the correct position for adding the next row. If using an odd number, you will automatically spiral up to the next row.

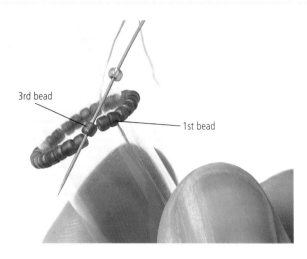

3rd bead

1st bead

step 3 Pick up another bead, then take the needle through the third bead along from the start of the first row. Pull slightly so that the new bead sits neatly on top of the second bead in row 1. Continue in this way until you arrive back at the first bead.

step 1 Thread an even number of beads onto the thread and tie it around a tubular object with a double knot, leaving a tiny gap between the first and last bead in the circle (do not overlap the beads or the stitch will not lie correctly and it will be impossible to work).

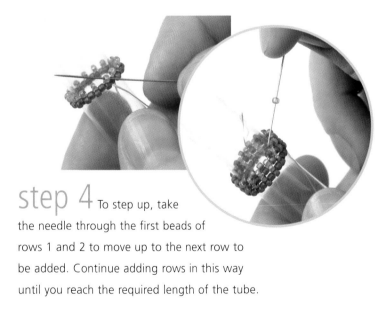

step 4 To step up, take the needle through the first beads of rows 1 and 2 to move up to the next row to be added. Continue adding rows in this way until you reach the required length of the tube.

step 2

Thread the needle and take it back through the first bead.

CIRCULAR PEYOTE

This variation of peyote produces a flat, circular piece of beading that is ideal for making lids or covering the base of vessels. It helps if you use two different colours of bead when first trying this technique. This will highlight each new row, allowing you to follow the pattern of the beads more easily. As with even-count tubular peyote, you will need to step up at the end of each row before adding a new row of beads.

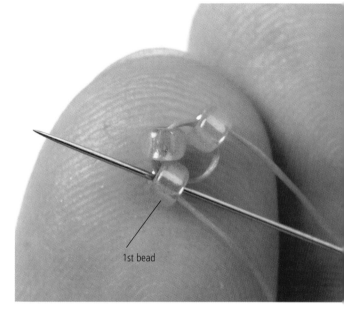

1st bead

step 2 To start row 2, step up by threading the needle through the first bead on row 1.

step 1 Thread a beading needle with 1m (1yd) of beading thread. Slide three beads to within 15cm (6in) of the tail end of the thread. Thread the needle through the three beads once more to form a circle.

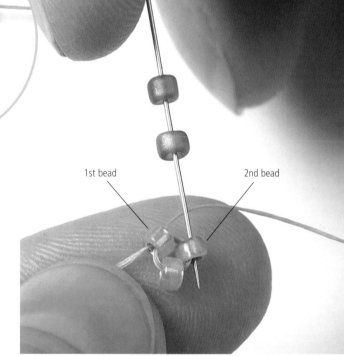

1st bead   2nd bead

step 3 Pick up two more beads, then take the needle through the second bead on row 1. Continue in this way, adding two beads between each pair of beads on row 1. You should add a total of six beads on row 2.

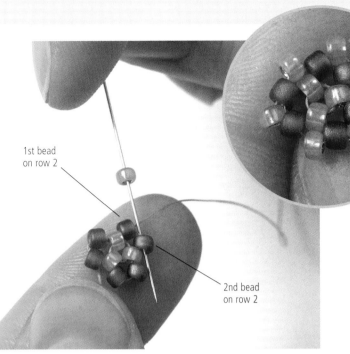

1st bead
on row 2

2nd bead
on row 2

step 4 For row 3, step up by threading
the needle through the first bead of the first
pair added on row 2. Pick up another bead,
then take the needle through the next bead
along on row 2. Continue adding a single bead
between all the beads on row 2. You should add
a total of six beads on row 3.

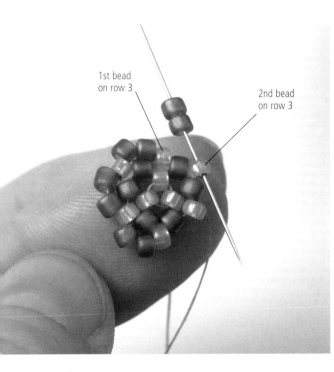

1st bead
on row 3

2nd bead
on row 3

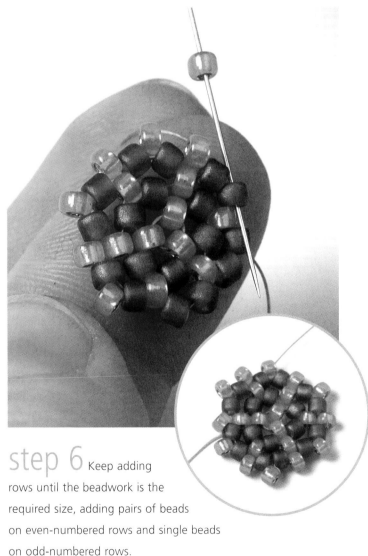

step 5 For row 4, step up by threading the needle
hrough the first bead added on row 3. Pick up two more beads,
hen take the needle through the next bead along on row 3.
Continue adding two beads between all the beads on row 3.
You should add a total of 12 beads on row 4.

step 6 Keep adding
rows until the beadwork is the
required size, adding pairs of beads
on even-numbered rows and single beads
on odd-numbered rows.

There are several ways to start and finish off threads, and everyone has their favourite. Some bead workers prefer not to make any knots, instead choosing to weave the ends backwards and forwards until the thread appears to be secure. Others prefer to tie a discrete knot, feeling that the beadwork seems more secure this way. Try different methods and work with the one that suits you best.

STARTING A THREAD

Always attach a new length of working thread before you finish off the old thread, because it can be difficult to see where the new thread needs to be positioned without the help of the old one.

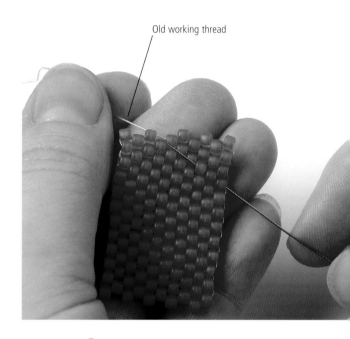

Old working thread

step 2 Bring the newly threaded needle up six to eight beads diagonally back from the bead from which the old thread emerges. Thread the needle through the first three or four beads in the direction of the old working thread, leaving a tail of about 15cm (6in).

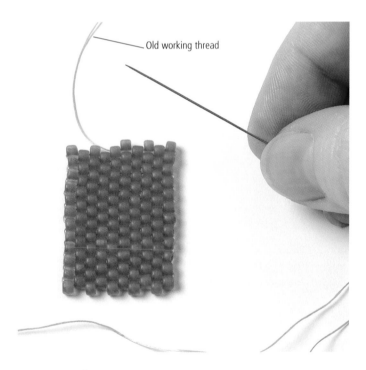

Old working thread

step 1 When the working thread is down to about 15cm (6in) long, remove the needle. Thread the needle with a new length of thread, ready to join into the beadwork.

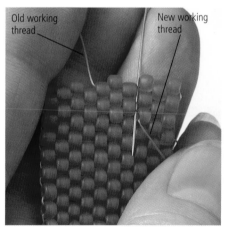

Old working thread

New working thread

step 3 Bring the needle out of the beadwork and then slip it underneath the thread between the nearest pair of beads.

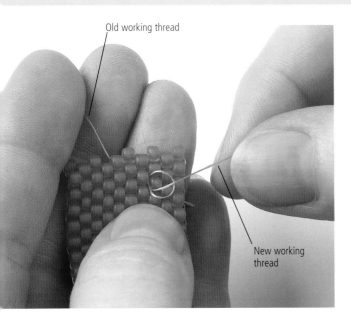

Old working thread

New working thread

step 4
Double knot the new thread by tying one single knot over another.

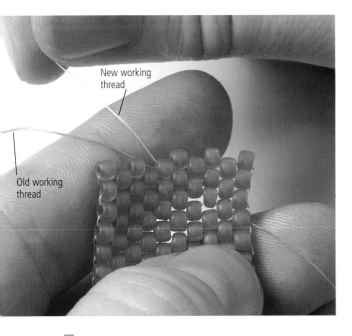

New working thread

Old working thread

step 5
Pass the needle through the next three or four beads, including the bead the old thread is coming out of. Give the thread a slight pull. As you do so, you will either feel or hear a slight click as the knot is pulled inside the next bead, concealing it neatly.

FINISHING A THREAD

When you have joined a new length of working thread, you need to finish off the old one. Any other loose threads, such as the tail end at the start of a piece of beadwork, also need to be tidied up in the same way when the beadwork is complete.

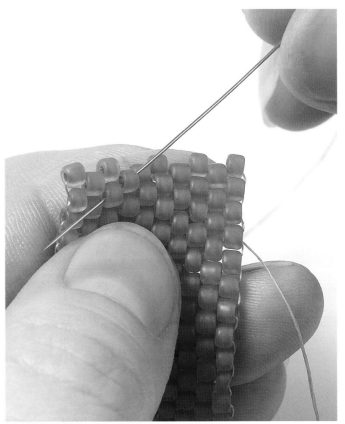

step 6
Rethread the old working thread through the needle. Take the needle through three or four beads in the opposite diagonal direction from the new thread you have just added. Double knot the thread as before, take it through another three or four beads, then click the knot into place. Cut off any excess thread.

Project 1: SEASHORE BRACELET

The base of this bracelet is made from triangle beads using flat even-count peyote stitch. Triangle beads slot together very well and reflect light beautifully. Embellishment, of course, is the key element in this bracelet, providing a great opportunity for you to indulge your creative side.

TOOLS AND MATERIALS

- 15g size 10 triangle beads: brown
- 5g size 11 seed beads: green
- 5g size 11 seed beads: peach
- 5g size 11 seed beads: brown
- 5 shell accent beads
- Two-bar clasp
- Beading thread: ash
- Beading needle
- Beading mat
- Scissors

MAKING THE BASE

step 1 Using eight triangle beads as a starting point, work a length of peyote stitch long enough to fit around the wrist, allowing about 1.5cm (⅝in) for the clasp (see Even-count peyote, page 28).

step 2 When the bracelet foundation is complete, attach the clasp (see Bar clasps, page 100). Finish off the loose ends of thread (see Finishing a thread, page 35).

ADDING EMBELLISHMENT

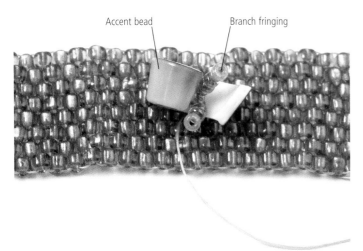

Accent bead   Branch fringing

Branch fringing

step 3 With the bracelet lying flat on a beading mat, experiment with the shell accent beads to see where they look best. When you are happy with the result, sew the central shell into position. Add some branch fringing to the centre of the shell using green seed beads for each branch, with a single peach seed bead at the tip for highlighting (see page 103).

step 4 Starting from underneath the base of the shell, add some more branch fringing. Use brown seed beads for each branch, with a single peach bead at the tip for highlighting. Vary the length of the branches to produce a pleasing design.

step 5 Continue adding fringing all around the base of the shell. Repeat this process with each of the remaining shells to complete the bracelet. Finish off any loose ends of thread as before.

THE THICK BUNCHES OF BRANCH FRINGING ECHO FRONDS OF SEAWEED IN THIS SEA-THEMED BRACELET, HELPING TO GIVE MOVEMENT AND TEXTURE TO THE PIECE.

Project 2: SEASHORE AMULET PURSE

The unusual colour of the pearl slices, and their rough shape and finish, are reminiscent of a section of shell washed up on the shore. In contrast to the extravagant fringing around the base, the main body of the purse is kept relatively simple, with only a single pearl slice as adornment. The strap is made from a single strand of seed beads, with a small section of fringing echoing that on the base of the purse.

MAKING THE PURSE

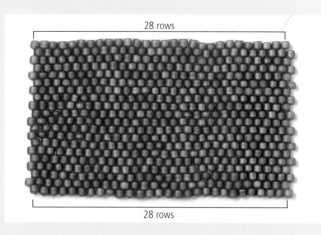

28 rows

28 rows

step 1 Using 20 size 8 seed beads as a starting point, work 28 rows of peyote stitch (see Even-count peyote, page 28). To check that you have completed the correct number of rows, count down the sides of the rectangle. There should be 28 beads on each side. If there are 28 on one side and 27 on the other, you need to work one more row.

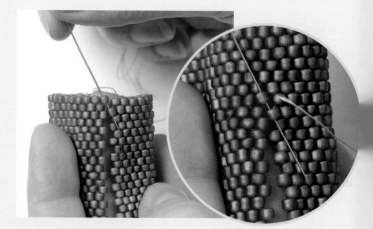

step 2 Fold the beadwork in half lengthways and pull the ends together so that the beads interlock. Stitch together through the beads, zigzagging back and forth from one side to the other. Zigzag back in the opposite direction to make the seam really secure. This is the side seam of the purse.

14 rows

step 3 Flatten the beadwork so that there are 14 beads each at the front and back of the purse. Stitch together through the loops of thread, not the beads. This creates the bottom seam of the purse. Finish off the loose ends of thread (see Finishing a thread, page 35).

ADDING THE BASE FRINGE

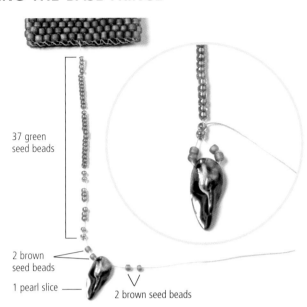

37 green
seed beads

2 brown
seed beads

1 pearl slice

2 brown seed beads

step 4 Bring the needle out at either of the two central beads at the base of the purse, ready to work the longest fringe (see Adding a fringe, page 102). Using size 11 seed beads, thread on 37 green seed beads, 2 brown seed beads, 1 pearl slice and 2 brown seed beads, then thread back up through the last 2 green seed beads added.

2 beads
between
branches

step 5 Work branch fringing all the way back up the initial beads, spacing them two green beads apart and using two green seed beads topped with a brown bead for each branch (see Branch fringing, page 103). Work two more branch fringes with a pearl slice at the base on either side of the central fringe, shortening the length of the fringes as you work outwards.

Accent-topped fringe

Small
branch

step 6 At each end of the base of the purse, work five shorter fringes using brown seed beads. End each fringe with an amber accent bead topped with a green seed bead, and add smaller branches using two green seed beads topped with a brown seed bead.

step 7 Extend the fringe up the left side of the purse by passing the needle through the beads in the actual body of the purse to the required position for each fringe. Position five amber-topped brown fringes near the bottom and several brown-topped green fringes a little further up. Sew a pearl slice to the centre front of the purse.

ATTACHING THE STRAP

step 8 Thread a beading needle with 1.5m (5ft) of beading thread. Flatten the purse at the top so that there is a pair of seed beads at each side. Bring the needle up through the front seed bead at one side of the purse. Using size 11 brown seed beads, thread on enough beads for the length of the strap required. Take the needle down through the front seed bead on the opposite side of the purse.

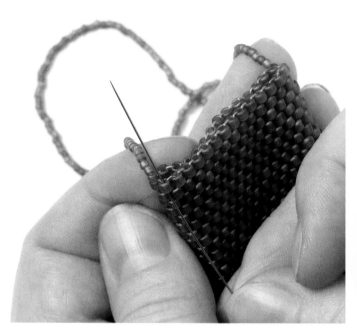

step 9 Turn the needle and bring the thread up through the back seed bead of the pair to secure the strap.

10th bead

step 10 Thread on nine more brown beads, then pass the needle through the tenth bead up on the original strap. Continue threading the needle through all the beads on the strap until you reach the last 10 beads on the other side of the strap.

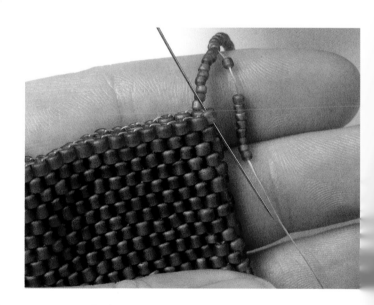

step 11 Thread on nine more beads, then pass the needle down through the back seed bead to mirror the other side of the strap.

EMBELLISHING THE STRAP

step 12 Work a small amount of branch fringing into the strap, extending down onto the top right corner of the purse. Add a fringe edging around the top of the purse by coming up through each bead at the edge of the purse, threading on two size 11 green seed beads and one size 11 brown seed bead. Take the needle around the brown bead, through the green beads, and then through the bead on the purse. Bring the needle up through the next bead along the edge of the purse, ready to add the next branch. Finish off any loose ends of thread as before.

USING MATT BEADS FOR THE PURSE ALLOWS THE IRIDESCENT PEARL SLICES TO STAND OUT. THEY ALSO PROVIDE EFFECTIVE HIGHLIGHTS AT THE ENDS OF THE SHINY-BEAD FRINGING.

Technique: BRICK STITCH

Brick stitch is a more solid stitch than many of the other widely used beadwork techniques. If you look at a flat piece of brick stitch, you will see that it resembles a brick wall, hence the name. Brick stitch is often used in its tubular form to create amulet purses, and since it is a fairly firm stitch, it can also be used to create freestanding beadwork, such as vessels and three-dimensional pieces. Brick stitch is best worked with a single strand of thread because the thread passes through each bead twice.

Getting the tension right

To keep the tension firm, pull the working thread back towards you and the tail end of the thread. If you pull the thread away from the beadwork, the tension will slacken and the beads will become too spaced. However, be careful not to pull the thread too strongly or the beadwork will overtighten and become wavy.

MAKING A LADDER

The first stage in working brick stitch is to form a foundation row, known as a ladder. Many amulet purses have a bugle ladder top.

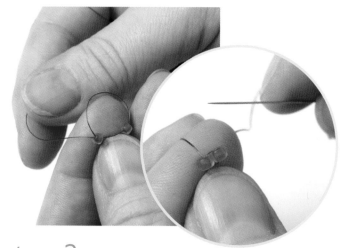

step 2 Pull the ends of the thread in opposite directions so that the beads click together snugly side by side.

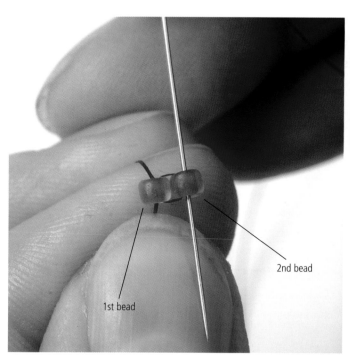

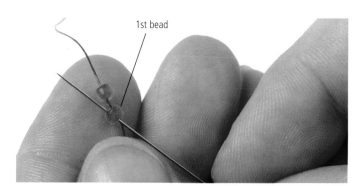

1st bead

step 1 Thread a beading needle with 1.5m (5ft) of beading thread. Thread two beads down to within 15cm (6in) of the tail end of the thread, then bring the needle back through the first bead.

2nd bead

1st bead

step 3 Holding the beads between a thumbnail and forefinger, take the needle back down through the second bead once again.

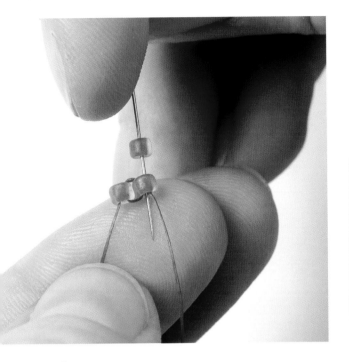

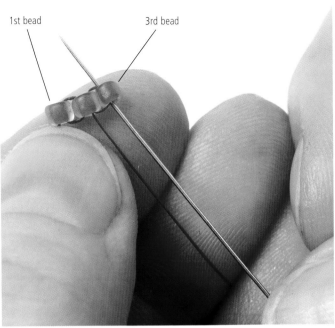

step 4 Pick up a bead and take the needle back down
through the second bead added. Pull the thread through and
down towards the tail end until the third bead sits next to the
second bead.

step 5 Thread the needle back up through the third
bead so that it is in the correct position to add the next bead.

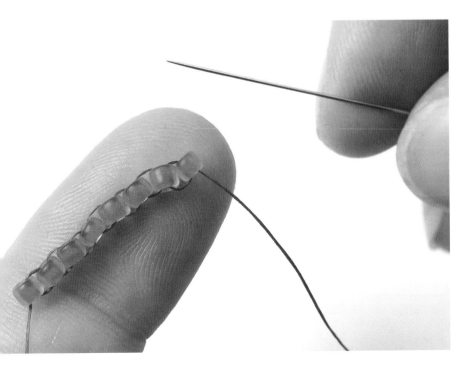

step 6 Continue adding beads
in this way until you reach the required
length. Notice that you are alternating
between taking the needle through the
top and bottom of the previous bead
added. Remember not to thread the
needle through the hole from which
the working thread is emerging.

ADDING MORE ROWS

Once the foundation ladder is complete, you can start adding rows of brick stitch.

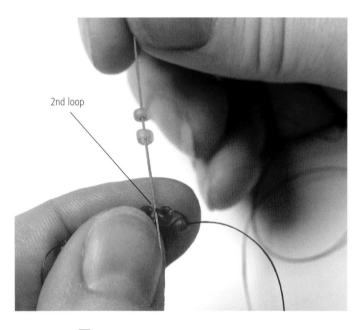

2nd loop

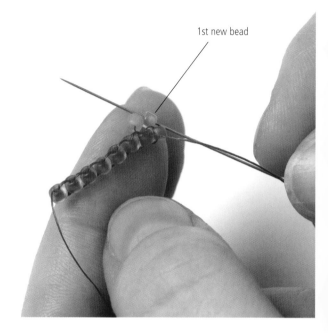

1st new bead

step 7 To start row 2, the thread should be coming out of the top of the last bead added to the ladder. Pick up two beads and take the needle through the second loop of thread along the ladder, from back to front.

step 8 Allowing the two new beads to sit side by side with the holes facing upwards, take the needle back up through the first new bead.

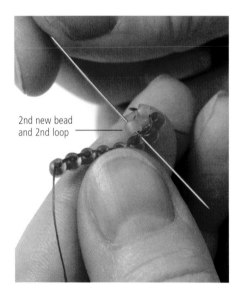

2nd new bead
and 2nd loop

step 9

Take the needle back down through the second new bead, then under the loop of the ladder once more.

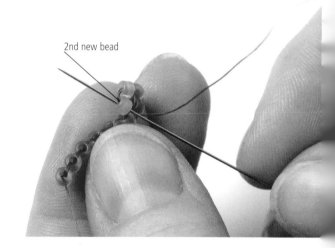

2nd new bead

step 10 Take the needle back up through the second bead again. These moves at the beginning of each row form a locking stitch that will help to anchor the first bead and stop it from tipping inwards so that you achieve a flat, even piece of beadwork.

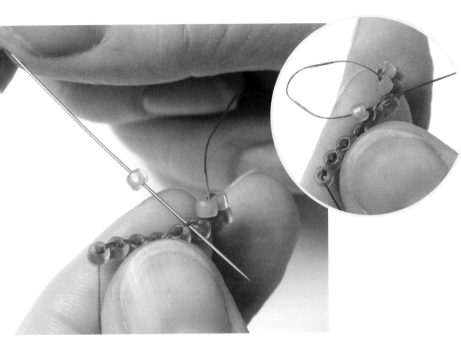

step 11
Pick up a third bead and take the needle under the next loop along on the ladder. Pull the thread through the loop until the new bead sits next to the other two beads added on this row.

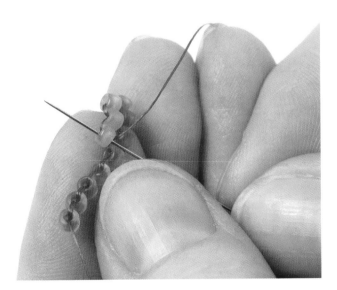

step 12
Thread the needle back up through the third bead, gently pulling upwards until all three beads sit in a row. Continue in this way, adding one bead at a time along the row.

step 13
To work row 3, turn the beadwork over so that the working end of the thread is nearest your fingertips. Add two new beads at the beginning of the row as before, threading the needle under the last loop of row 2. Continue adding single beads along the rest of the row. Add subsequent rows in this way until the beadwork reaches the required length.

INCREASING

This technique can be used to increase as many beads as you wish on the outside edge of the beadwork.

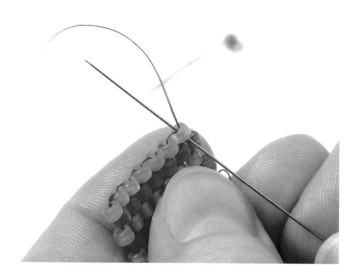

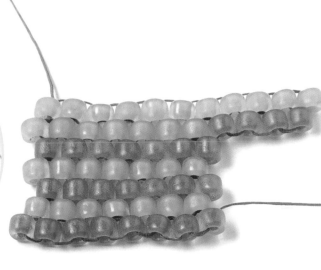

step 2 Take the needle back down through the bead just added.

step 1 When you reach a point where you require an increase, thread on one bead, then go back up through the bead from which the thread is emerging.

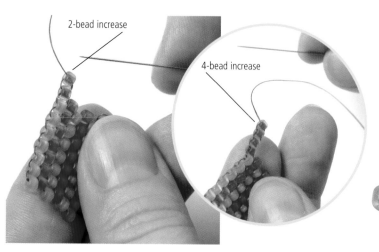

step 3 Add another increase bead in the same way. Continue adding beads until you have increased by the required amount.

step 4 Continue to work the next row in brick stitch, working across the increase beads and then the rest of the previous row.

DECREASING

Use this method to decrease beads on the outside edge of the beadwork. In this example, a ladder of seven beads is being decreased symmetrically to a point.

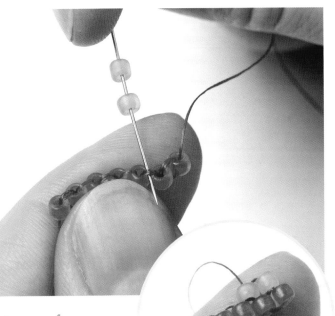

step 1 After working the ladder (see page 42), start row 2 by adding two beads, threading the needle under the second loop in from the end of the ladder (see Adding more rows, page 44). Secure the beads in the usual way, then continue along the row, adding one bead at a time.

step 2 To start row 3, add two beads in the same way as before, threading the needle under the second loop in from the end of row 2. Complete the row, adding one bead at a time.

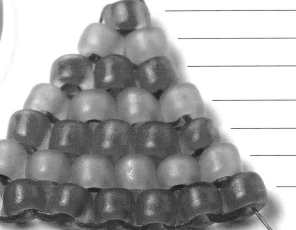

Row 7 = 1 bead
Row 6 = 2 beads
Row 5 = 3 beads
Row 4 = 4 beads
Row 3 = 5 beads
Row 2 = 6 beads
Row 1 = 7 beads

step 3 As you add more rows, starting each row by threading the needle under the second loop in from the end of the previous row when adding the first pair of beads, the beadwork will decrease down to a point. You could then thread back down through the beadwork to one of the outside beads on the ladder row and repeat this process on the other side to create a diamond shape.

Project 3: VICTORIAN CHOKER

This choker is guaranteed to bring a touch of elegance to any outfit. The neck band of bugle beads is softened by a central fringe that drapes beautifully. The neck band is a great way to familiarize yourself with making the ladder that is used to start brick stitch.

MAKING THE NECK BAND

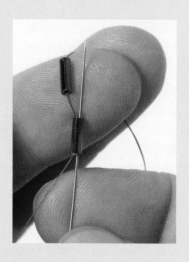

step 1
Thread a beading needle with 1m (1yd) of beading thread. Start the ladder by passing two bugle beads down to within 15cm (6in) of the tail end of the thread. Bring the needle back through the first bead.

step 2
Continue adding bugle beads until you have the required length of ladder, allowing about 1.5cm (⅝in) for the clasp (see Making a ladder, page 42).

ADDING THE FRINGE

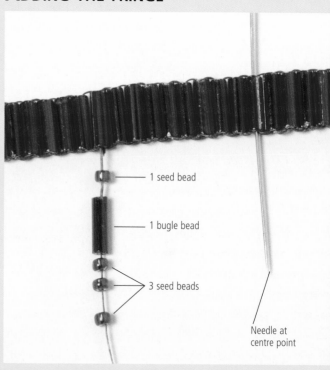

- 1 seed bead
- 1 bugle bead
- 3 seed beads
- Needle at centre point

step 3
Fold the bugle ladder in half to determine where the centre is. The fringe consists of 17 strands that increase in length symmetrically towards the centre. In this instance, the use of bugle beads dictates the length of the shortest strand, so this strand is added first instead of starting at the centre, which is usually recommended (see Adding a fringe, page 102). Count eight bugles out from the centre bead, then pass the needle down through that bugle. Thread on one seed bead, one bugle bead and three seed beads.

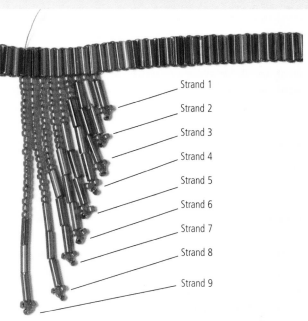

Strand 1
Strand 2
Strand 3
Strand 4
Strand 5
Strand 6
Strand 7
Strand 8
Strand 9

step 4 Skipping the last

three seed beads added, pass the needle back up through the bugle and seed bead, then up through the bugle bead in the ladder from which the fringe is emerging. Gently pull the thread so that the seed bead sits snugly against the bugle in the ladder.

step 6 Continue to add seven

more fringes, adding the following beads:

Strand 3: 1 seed, 3 bugles, 3 seeds.
Strand 4: 4 seeds, 3 bugles, 3 seeds.
Strand 5: 8 seeds, 3 bugles, 3 seeds.
Strand 6: 12 seeds, 3 bugles, 3 seeds.
Strand 7: 16 seeds, 3 bugles, 3 seeds.
Strand 8: 21 seeds, 3 bugles, 3 seeds.
Strand 9: 23 seeds, 3 bugles, 3 seeds.

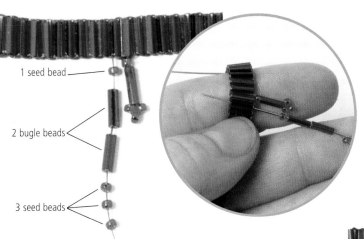

1 seed bead

2 bugle beads

3 seed beads

step 5 Pass the needle down through the next bugle

towards the centre of the ladder. Thread on one seed bead, two bugles and three seed beads. Skipping the last three seed beads added, pass the needle back up through the remaining beads and then through the ladder bugle from which the fringe is hanging. Take the needle back down through the next bugle towards the centre of the ladder.

step 7 When strand 9 is completed at the centre of the

choker, add another eight strands on the other side, making sure they reduce in length symmetrically to the first side. When the fringe is complete, attach the clasp (see page 98), then finish off the loose ends of thread (see Finishing a thread, page 35).

THIS CHOKER HAS BEEN CREATED ENTIRELY IN BRIGHT RED BEADS FOR A DRAMATIC EFFECT, BUT YOU COULD USE A VARIETY OF BEAD COLOURS IN THE DESIGN IF YOU WISH.

Project 4: VICTORIAN EARRINGS

These earrings match the choker featured on the previous pages. They are made up of monocolour bugle and seed beads to give a simple but stylish look, but you could use a variety of colour combinations for a different effect. Think also about combining matt with shiny beads.

MAKING THE BASE

step 1 Using 0.5m (1½ft) of beading thread, make a ladder of five bugle beads (see Making a ladder, page 42).

step 2 Add a second row of four bugle beads (see Adding more rows, page 44).

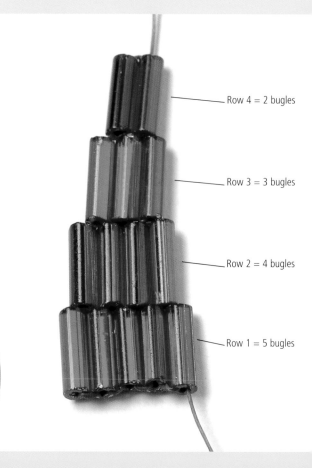

Row 4 = 2 bugles

Row 3 = 3 bugles

Row 2 = 4 bugles

Row 1 = 5 bugles

step 3 Add another two rows in the same way, using three bugles in the third row and two bugles in the fourth (see Decreasing, page 47).

ATTACHING THE FINDING

step 4
Thread on one seed bead, then pass the needle through the loop on one of the earring findings. Thread the needle back down through the seed bead, then through the other bugle of the top pair. This makes the finding sit well between the two bugles. Thread back up and around the finding again to give added strength.

ADDING THE FRINGE

1 seed bead ⎯⎯
1 bugle bead ⎯⎯
3 seed beads ⎯⎯

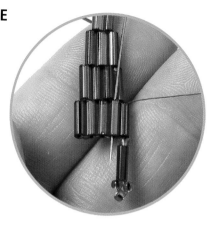

step 5
When the finding is secure, thread down to either end of the base bugles, ready to add the fringe (see Adding a fringe, page 110). Thread on one seed bead, one bugle, then three seed beads. Skipping the last three seed beads added, thread back up through the bugle and remaining seed bead, then back into the bugle on the ladder. Pass the needle down through the next bugle in the row, ready to add the second strand.

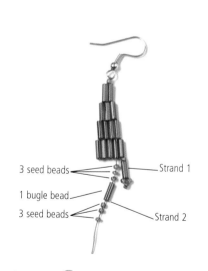

3 seed beads ⎯⎯⎯ Strand 1
1 bugle bead ⎯⎯
3 seed beads ⎯⎯ Strand 2

step 6
Thread on: three seeds, one bugle, three seeds. Skipping the last three seed beads added, thread back up as before, then down through the third bugle on the ladder.

Strand 3 has 6 seed beads at the top

step 7
Add the central strand, using six seeds, one bugle and three seeds. Thread back up as before, then pass the needle down through the fourth bugle. Add the fourth strand to match the second, and the fifth strand to match the first, so that you have symmetrical fringing at the bottom of the earring. Finish off any loose ends of thread (see Finishing a thread, page 35). Make a matching earring in the same way.

THE THREE BEADS AT THE ENDS OF THE FRINGING COULD BE REPLACED WITH TINY ACCENT BEADS. THESE WOULD ATTRACT ATTENTION AS THE FRINGE MOVES WHEN WORN.

Technique: SQUARE STITCH

Square stitch beadwork looks similar to loomwork but has the advantage that there are fewer ends of thread to finish off. Square stitch also produces hard-wearing pieces because the thread travels through each bead several times, almost creating a fabric of its own. This stitch is excellent for creating patterns because the beads sit in grid formation. Cross-stitch patterns can be worked to stunning effect – just follow them as you would if stitching – or create your own designs using graph paper and coloured pencils. Square stitch is best worked with a single strand of thread because the thread passes through each bead several times.

Getting the tension right

It is relatively easy to keep the tension correct with square stitch. Use a stop bead to keep the thread straight on the first two rows. Once you have been through these rows again with the thread to straighten them, the subsequent rows will sit right.

WORKING SQUARE STITCH

Cylinder beads are ideal for square stitch because they are uniform and sit neatly side by side. They also have fairly large holes, making it easier to accommodate the amount of thread that passes through each bead.

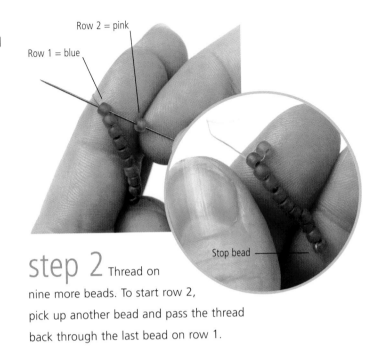

Row 2 = pink
Row 1 = blue
Stop bead

step 2 Thread on nine more beads. To start row 2, pick up another bead and pass the thread back through the last bead on row 1.

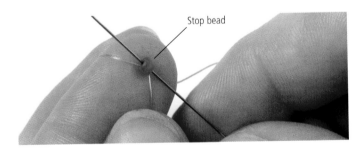

Stop bead

step 1 Thread a beading needle with 1.5m (5ft) of beading thread. Pick up a bead and slide it to within 15cm (6in) of the tail end of the thread. Bring the needle back up through the bead, creating a loop around the bead. This is called a stop bead.

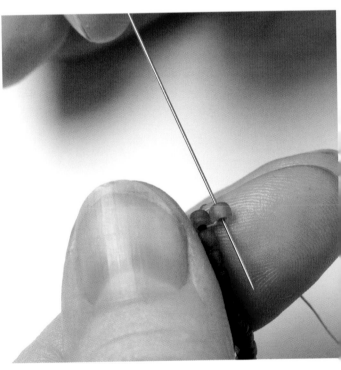

step 3 Take the needle back through the bead just added to start off row 2.

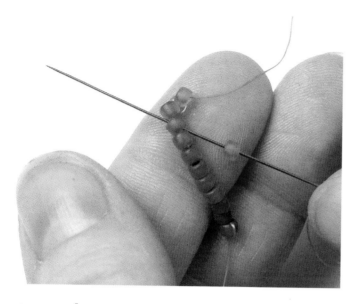

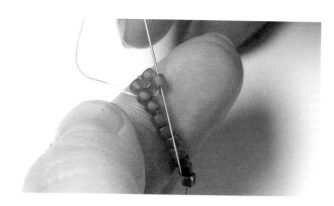

step 5
Thread the needle back through the bead just added on row 2. Continue along the row in this way.

step 4
Pick up another bead and take the needle back through the next to last bead on row 1.

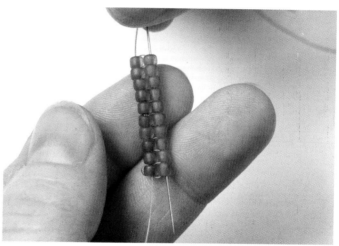

step 7
Turn the needle and take it back through the second row of beads. Pull the thread through so that the two rows sit neatly together. Continue adding rows in this way.

step 6
At this point, the beads may seem to be sitting slightly unevenly. To secure them together, pass the needle back through the first row of beads. Pull the thread through.

BEADER'S TIP
Square stitch involves passing the thread through the beads several times, so it is a good idea to use thread conditioner. There are several types, from synthetic to natural conditioners such as beeswax, that help to prevent the thread from splitting and wearing. If the needle gets stuck, use flat nose pliers to help pull it through, but do not pull too firmly or the bead can shatter.

INCREASING

Shaping techniques allow you to produce intricate shapes, such as butterflies and flowers. This method allows you to increase beads on either of the outside edges of the work.

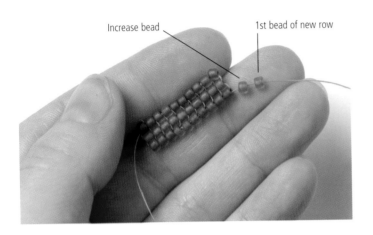

Increase bead

1st bead of new row

step 1 Bring the needle through the last bead on the row you wish to increase. Thread on one more bead (the increase bead) plus the first bead of the next row.

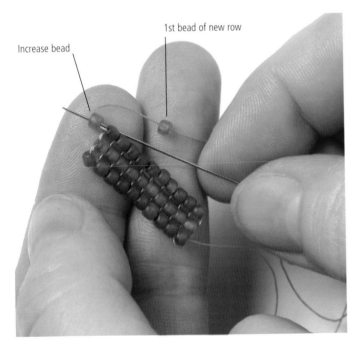

Increase bead

1st bead of new row

step 2 Skipping the last bead added, thread the needle back through the increase bead.

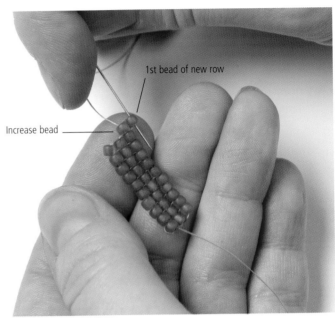

1st bead of new row

Increase bead

step 3 Thread the needle through the first bead of the new row (the last bead added).

step 4 Continue working square stitch along the row. Note that you can add as many beads as you wish for an increase, then simply square stitch your way back into the main section of the beadwork to secure.

DECREASING

As with increasing, decreasing is also fairly straightforward in square stitch. This technique allows you to decrease beads on the outside edge of the work.

step 2
Thread on a bead, go back through the bead the thread is coming out of, then back through the bead just added.

step 1
When you finish the row just before the one you need to decrease, thread back as usual through the previous row and then through the row just added. However, instead of taking the needle through to the end of this row, bring it out where you wish the decrease to begin.

step 3
Continue along the row until you reach the bead where you wish to stop the row. Secure the beads in the usual way and continue adding rows of square stitch.

TUBULAR SQUARE STITCH

Tubular square stitch is easier to master when worked around
a cylinder, such as a drinking straw, pen or plastic tube.
This technique can be used to create rope necklaces, tubes
and vessels.

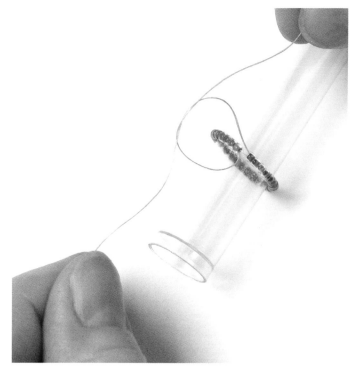

step 1 Using a 1m (1yd) length of beading thread,
thread on as many beads as necessary to fit around the cylinder.

step 3 Place the circle of beads around the cylinder
again. Pull the ends of the thread in opposite directions to
tighten the beads firmly together, then tie the thread in a double
knot to secure into place.

step 2 Remove the
beads from the cylinder and pass the
needle through the beads a few at a time
from the tail end upwards, leaving the beads
in a loose circle.

step 4 Thread the needle through the first bead of row 1.

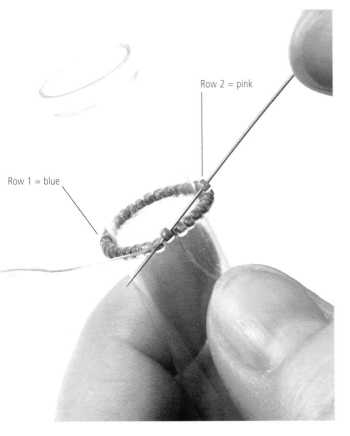

Row 2 = pink

Row 1 = blue

step 5
Pick up the first bead of row 2, then thread the needle through the first bead of row 1 again.

step 6
Thread the needle through the first bead of row 2 again. Notice that you are working anticlockwise. Continue adding beads all around row 2 in this way.

step 7
When the row is complete, take the thread through all the beads on row 2 once more, then bring the needle out through the first bead added on row 2. Add a third row of beads in the same way, but this time work clockwise around the cylinder. Add as many rows as required, working anticlockwise on even-numbered rows and clockwise on odd-numbered rows.

Project 5: RAINBOW BRACELET

This bracelet uses the colours of the rainbow in a zigzag pattern. Refer to the colour wheel on page 22 to help select a palette of colours, choosing the primary colours first and then filling in the gaps. Keep trying different tints and shades of each colour until you are happy with the overall effect.

TOOLS AND MATERIALS

- 10g size 11 seed beads: 12 rainbow colours
- Two 8mm beads: yellow
- Beading thread: ash
- Beading needle
- Beading mat
- Scissors
- Flat nose pliers

MAKING THE BASE

step 1 Starting at the top left corner of the chart on page 59, thread the first 19 seed beads onto a 1m (1yd) length of beading thread to form the first row of the bracelet. Check that the colours are in the same order in which they appear on the chart.

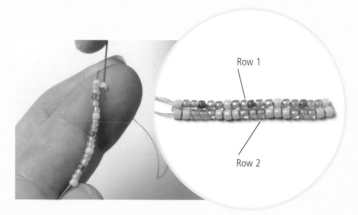

Row 1

Row 2

step 2 Add the second row of beads using square stitch (see page 52), remembering to change colour as indicated on the chart. You may find it useful to place a sheet of white paper on the chart just below the row you are working on to avoid confusion.

step 3 Work down the chart, changing colours as required. When you reach the end of the chart, repeat from the top again until the bracelet is long enough to fit around the wrist, allowing about 1.5cm (⅝in) for the fastener.

MAKING THE FASTENER

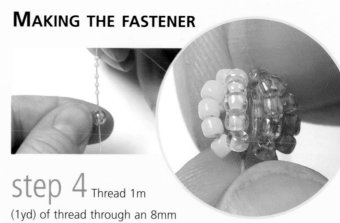

step 4 Thread 1m (1yd) of thread through an 8mm bead and tie it with a double knot, leaving a 15cm (6in) tail. Thread on five yellow seed beads, then pass the needle through the 8mm bead so that the yellow beads loop around the larger bead. Continue adding strings of seed beads until the central bead is fully covered, following a rainbow colour order. Make a second embellished bead in the same way. Finish off the loose ends of thread on all the pieces (see Finishing a thread, page 35).

step 5
To add the embellished beads, bring the needle with 1m (1yd) of thread out of the fifth bead on the end row of the bracelet. Thread on one seed bead of any colour, then take the thread through one of the embellished beads. Add a second seed bead of the same colour as the first one. Skipping this second seed bead, take the needle down through the embellished bead, the first seed bead and then through the fifth bead on the bracelet again. Repeat this journey two or three times for extra strength. Add the second embellished bead in the same way, five beads from the other edge (see Bead and loop fasteners, page 101).

step 6
To add the loops, bring the needle with 1m (1yd) of thread out through the fifth bead on the opposite end of the bracelet. Thread on 21 seed beads in rainbow colour order, then take the needle back down through the first bead added to create a loop. Thread the needle through the fifth bead on the bracelet again, then repeat this journey two or three times for extra strength. Add a second beaded loop in the same way, five beads from the other edge. Finish off any loose ends of thread as before.

BEADER'S TIP

Seed beads are not always exactly the same size, so check that the fastening loop fits over the embellished 8mm bead before securing the loop to the bracelet. Use more or fewer beads if required to produce a snug fit, remembering that beading thread only gives a small amount.

Start from here, then repeat from this point until bracelet reaches required length

IT IS EASY TO CREATE YOUR OWN UNIQUE BEADING DESIGN USING GRAPH PAPER AND COLOURED PENCILS, THEN COLOUR MATCH THE BEADS TO THE DRAWING.

Project 6: RAINBOW NECKLACE

This necklace can be worn with the strands twisted or gently draped around the neck. One of the main features of the necklace is the end caps, which create a wonderfully neat but decorative finish. As with the matching bracelet on the previous pages, use the colour wheel on page 22 to help you select a rainbow colour palette.

TOOLS AND MATERIALS

- 10g size 11 seed beads: 12 rainbow colours
- Two gold eyepins
- Two 1.5cm (4in) long gold end caps
- Lobster clasp and jump ring
- Beading thread: ash
- Beading needle
- 1cm (⅜in) cylinder to bead around, such as an empty bead tube
- Beading mat
- Scissors
- Clear nail polish
- Cutting pliers
- Round nose pliers

MAKING THE TUBE

step 1 Thread 24 beads onto 1m (1yd) of beading thread in rainbow colour order, leaving a 15cm (6in) tail end. Pass the needle from the tail end upwards through the 24 beads once again to form a circle.

step 2 Place the circle of beads around the cylinder. Pull the thread tight so that the beads sit firmly together, then tie the thread in a double knot to secure.

BEADER'S TIP

It is a good idea to lay out small piles of beads in the correct colour order on a beading mat. This will make beading a little quicker because you will not have to stop and think about which colour to add next.

step 3 Work a
second row of tubular
square stitch (see page 56).
You will be working
anticlockwise on this row, so in
order to make the colours swirl around the tube, each new bead
you add on row 2 should be the same colour as the bead that
sits to the left of the bead from which the thread emerges. As
you continue around the tube, you will see each pair of beads
in the same colour begin to create a diagonal stripe.

step 4 Continue to work tubular square stitch, adding
the colours in the correct order so that they spiral around the
tube. Work 22 rows in total. Finish off the loose ends of thread
(see Finishing a thread, page 35).

MAKING THE STRANDS

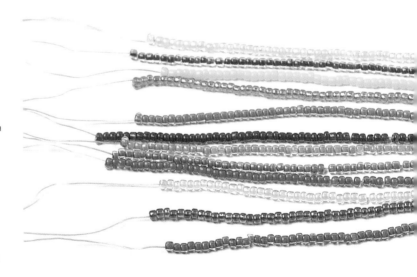

step 5 Decide what length you want the necklace to
be, allowing about 1.5cm (⅝in) for the clasp. If you are going to
twist the strands, allow a little extra length because twisting will
shorten the necklace slightly. Cut 12 pieces of beading thread to
this length, plus 30cm (12in) for finishing. Thread a seed bead
onto the thread, leaving a 15cm (6in) tail end. Pass the thread
through the bead once again to create a stop bead. Thread on
as many beads in the same colour as necessary to fill the thread,
leaving another 15cm (6in) tail at the other end.

step 6 Repeat until you have 12 strands of beads, one
in each colour of the rainbow.

ATTACHING THE CLASP

step 9 When the nail polish is thoroughly dry, cut the spare ends of threads as close to the knot as possible.

step 7 Thread the ends of the strands with no stop beads through an eyepin. Tie them onto the eyepin with a knot.

step 8 Tighten the knot as much as possible, then put a small dab of clear nail polish onto it for added strength.

step 10 At the other end of the strands, remove the loops from the stop beads by gently pushing the needle between the loop and stop bead and pulling the thread through. When they are all free, hold up all 12 ends vertically to see if you need to remove any beads from this end to make all the beading even. Attach this end to an eyepin as before.

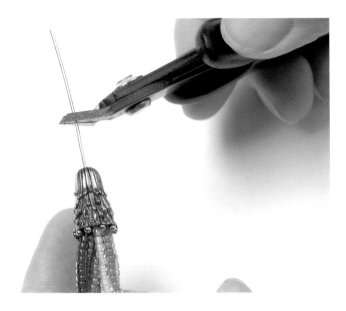

step 11
Thread an end cap onto one of the eye pins so that it covers all the messy ends of thread. Using cutting pliers, cut off the wire end just under halfway down.

step 12
Place a pair of round nose pliers directly above the end cap, then angle the wire towards you at 45 degrees. Move the pliers up towards the top of the wire and bend it around to form an open loop. If the wire is too long for the loop, cut off another small section.

step 13
Slip a lobster clasp onto the loop and squeeze the loop closed with the pliers. Add a jump ring to the other end of the necklace in the same way. Slide the tube onto the centre of the strands.

TWIST THE NECKLACE WHEN WEARING IT SO THAT THE STRANDS SWIRL AROUND TO MATCH THE PATTERN ON THE CENTRAL TUBE, OR LEAVE THEM STRAIGHT FOR CONTRAST.

Netting stitch produces open, lacy beadwork that drapes beautifully around the neck and wrist, but it can also be worked firmly enough to make a tube. The stitch is of slightly more limited use than other techniques, but it is still very effective. The thread pattern of netting stitch is quite involved and delicate, so it is almost always worked with one strand of thread. Using two strands could cause unnecessary knotting and make the overall netting a little too taut, losing much of the stitch's wonderful movement. However, use two strands to create a firmer base for freestanding and three-dimensional beadwork.

Getting the tension right

You may find it best to work this stitch flat on a bead mat so that you can see when the tension needs altering. If the tension is too loose, the thread will show; if it is too tight, the netting will buckle. Try not to pierce the working thread that is already sitting in the bead or there is a strong risk of the beadwork twisting on itself.

FIVE-BEAD NETTING

This forms the basis of all netting stitches, with just the number of beads varying. Two colours of beads are used here for clarity – turquoise (T) and pale green (G).

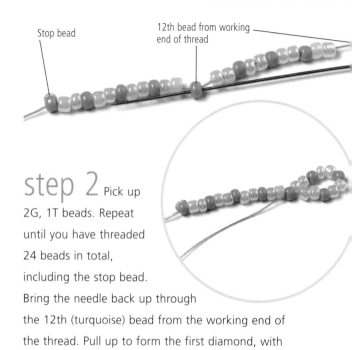

Stop bead

12th bead from working end of thread

step 2 Pick up 2G, 1T beads. Repeat until you have threaded 24 beads in total, including the stop bead. Bring the needle back up through the 12th (turquoise) bead from the working end of the thread. Pull up to form the first diamond, with a turquoise bead at all four points of the diamond.

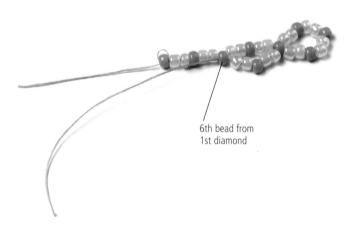

6th bead from 1st diamond

step 3 Thread 2G, 1T, 2G beads onto the needle. Bring the needle back up through the sixth (turquoise) bead along the first row, counting from the first diamond.

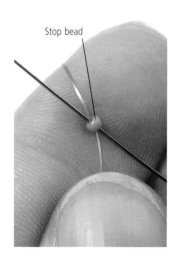

Stop bead

step 1 Thread a beading needle with 1m (1yd) of beading thread and pick up 1T bead. Slide the bead down to within 15cm (6in) of the tail end, then bring the needle back up through the bead to create a stop bead.

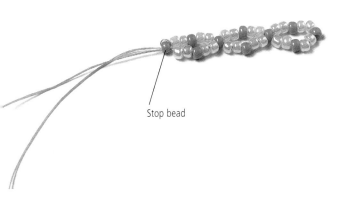

Stop bead

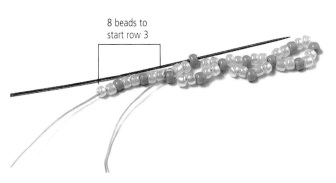

8 beads to start row 3

step 4 Make another diamond in the same way, finishing the row by taking the needle up through the stop bead.

step 5 Pick up 2G, 1T, 2G, 1T, 2G beads. Take the needle down through the middle turquoise bead of the last diamond on the previous row.

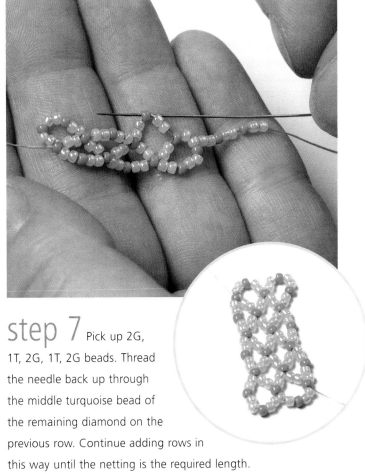

step 6 Pick up 2G, 1T, 2G beads. Take the needle down through the middle turquoise bead of the next diamond on the previous row, forming another diamond. Repeat to make a third diamond.

step 7 Pick up 2G, 1T, 2G, 1T, 2G beads. Thread the needle back up through the middle turquoise bead of the remaining diamond on the previous row. Continue adding rows in this way until the netting is the required length.

TUBULAR NETTING

This technique produces a tube of netting that makes effective necklaces and bracelets. Working one netted tube over another also produces an interesting effect. Work this stitch around a cylinder, such as a drinking straw, to help you keep the tension constant. Two colours of beads are used here for clarity – turquoise (T) and pale green (G).

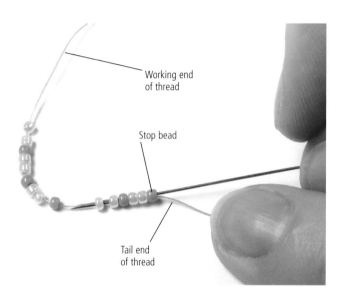

Working end of thread

Stop bead

Tail end of thread

step 1 Thread the needle with beads in the same way as for five-bead netting (see page 64), but thread only 15 beads in total. Pass the needle through all the beads once again, starting at the tail end.

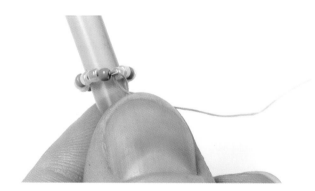

step 2 Place the circle of beads around a cylinder and tie the thread in a double knot.

Stop bead

step 3 Take the needle through the first turquoise bead (the stop bead) once again.

BEADER'S TIP

When changing thread, take care not to knot the threads too tightly or it will cause a dent in the tube that is impossible to get out. If possible, attach the new thread by threading up through the netting as near as possible to where you need to continue, make a double knot between two beads, then thread through to the required place. When you have worked about another 2cm (¾in) of the stitch, thread the old thread back up and finish in the usual way (see Finishing a thread, page 35).

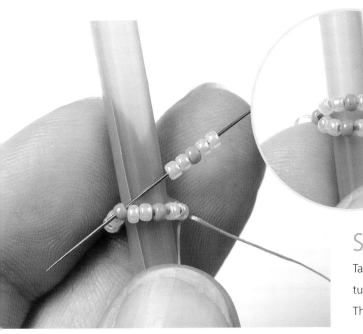

step 4 Pick up 2G, 1T, 2G beads. Take the needle through the second turquoise bead along on the original row. This forms the first diamond.

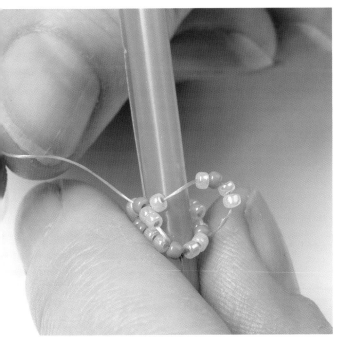

step 5 Add a second loop in the same way, then pick up 2G, 1T, 2G beads for the third loop. There will only be one turquoise bead left on the first row (the bead at the start of the row). To attach the third loop, you need to go through the turquoise bead in the middle of the first diamond you added.

step 6 Pick up 2G, 1T, 2G beads. Take the needle through the turquoise bead in the middle of the second diamond you added. This forms the first diamond of the new row. Note how the tube is spiralling upwards. Continue adding diamonds until the tube is the required length.

Project 7: SUMMER AMULET PURSE

A netted section of beadwork is reminiscent of a garden trellis. Intertwined with vines and flowers, it makes the perfect summer purse. The base is a net of seed beads with a ladder stitch bugle bead top, finished with a single string of beads as a strap. The surface embellishment of seed beads and flower accent beads transform the simple base into a delightful amulet purse.

MAKING THE PURSE BASE

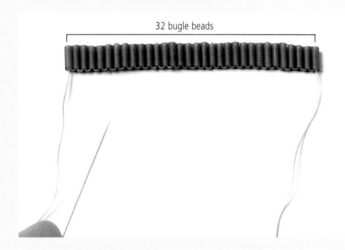

32 bugle beads

step 1 Thread a beading needle with 1.5m (5ft) of beading thread. Make a ladder of 32 bugle beads (see Making a ladder, page 42). Flip the ladder over so that the working thread is coming down through the first bugle on the left side.

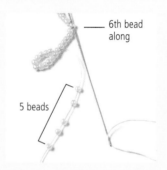

6th bead along

5 beads

step 3 Thread on five more pale green seed beads. Skipping the next five beads on the initial row, pass the needle through the sixth bead to form the second diamond.

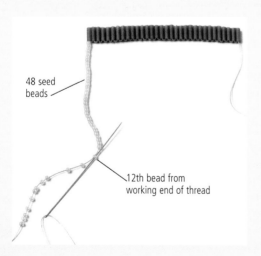

48 seed beads

12th bead from working end of thread

step 2 Thread on 48 pale green seed beads. Pass the needle up through the 12th bead along from the working end of the thread, pulling up the thread gently to form the first diamond (see Five-bead netting, page 64).

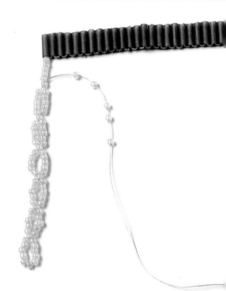

step 4 Continue adding sets of five beads and then threading through the sixth bead on the initial row until you reach the bugle ladder.

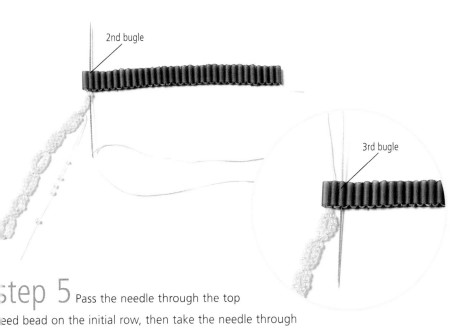

2nd bugle

3rd bugle

8 beads

step 5
Pass the needle through the top seed bead on the initial row, then take the needle through the next bugle. You will see that the first row of netting sits neatly beneath the first and second bugles on the ladder. Take the needle down through the third bugle.

step 7
When you reach the bottom of the row, you need to add eight beads. This will allow you to turn the needle in order to work the stitch back up the netting.

5 beads

step 6
To work the next row of netting, you only need to add three pale green seed beads to complete the first half diamond at the top of the row. Complete the remaining diamonds by adding five beads each time, threading through each central bead of the five added on the previous row.

step 8
Continue adding rows of netting stitch until you reach the next to last bugle. Work the next row of netting down the purse as before, but when you work the bottom diamond, use five beads instead of the usual eight. Bring the needle through the central bead of the bottom diamond on the other side of the purse, joining the two sides together.

step 9 Take a good look at the bead pattern to figure out where the two side edges need to be joined in order to maintain the netting pattern. Join the edges, adding two beads and then running the needle through the central beads of the diamonds on alternate edges to complete the pattern.

step 10 Make sure that the points at the base of the purse match front and back. When you are happy with the alignment, join the central beads at each pair of diamond points using square stitch (see page 52). Finish off the loose ends of thread (see Finishing a thread, page 35).

EMBELLISHING THE PURSE

step 11 Thread the needle down through the bugle at the top right side of the purse. Add a piece of branch fringing diagonally across the front of the purse from top right to bottom left using turquoise seed beads (see Branch fringing, page 102). Weave the fringe in and out of the netting at regular intervals to hold it in place.

step 12 Add side branches of three, four or five turquoise beads at intervals. Finish each side branch with a flower accent bead topped with a turquoise seed bead. Note that the fringing extends beyond the bottom edge of the purse. Add a couple more branch fringes extending diagonally outwards from the main fringe.

ADDING THE STRAP

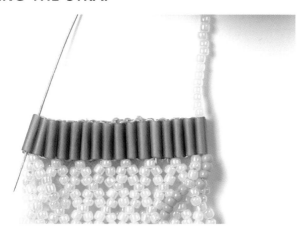

step 15 Embellish the right side of the strap with the same style of fringing as on the body of the purse. Finish off any loose ends of thread as before.

step 13 Flatten the purse at the top so that there is a pair of bugles at each side. Bring the needle up through the front bugle at one side of the purse. Thread on pale green seed beads until you reach the required length of strap. Pass the needle down through the front bugle on the opposite side of the purse.

21st bead

step 14 Take the needle up through the back bugle of the pair. Thread on 20 pale green seed beads, then pass the needle through the 21st bead up on the strap. Continue threading the needle through the beads of the strap until you reach 20 beads from the other end. Thread another 20 seed beads onto the needle, then take the needle down through the back bugle to mirror the other side of the strap.

THE BRANCH OF FLOWERS HAS BEEN WORKED IN TURQUOISE TO STAND OUT FROM THE PALE NETTING TRELLIS BUT WITHOUT BEING TOO DOMINANT.

Project 8: GARDEN LARIAT

A lariat is one continual piece of beadwork. It can be hung around the neck and casually knotted or doubled like a scarf with the flower ends pulled through the loop. Worked in two toning colours of seed beads, the bellflower accent beads at each end have the flower heads pointing upwards instead of the more usual downwards.

TOOLS AND MATERIALS

- 20g size 11 seed beads: green
- 20g size 11 seed beads: turquoise
- 16 bellflower accent beads: green
- Beading thread: ash
- Beading needle
- 6mm (¼in) cylinder to bead around, such as a drinking straw
- Beading mat
- Scissors

MAKING THE TUBE

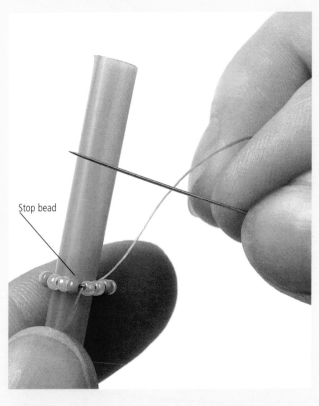

Stop bead

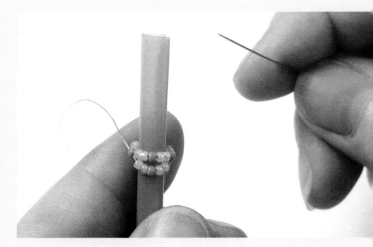

step 2
Pass the needle through the first turquoise seed bead once again, then pick up two green, one turquoise and two green beads. Skipping the next turquoise bead, pass the needle through the second turquoise bead.

step 1
Work a length of tubular netting in the usual way (see page 66), alternating 1 turquoise seed bead and then 2 green seed beads until you have 15 beads in total. Pass the needle through all 15 beads once again from the tail end upwards to form a circle. Place the bead circle over a cylinder and work a double knot between the first and last beads of the circle.

step 3
Continue adding loops of spiralling netting stitch until the tube is the desired length.

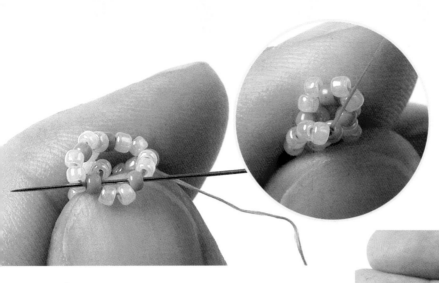

step 4
Thread the needle through the turquoise beads at the end of the tube, pull up into a circle, then tie a double knot to secure. Do not finish off the ends of thread.

EMBELLISHING THE TUBE

3 seed beads between pairs of accent beads

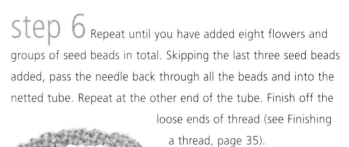

step 5
Thread on one bellflower accent bead, then one green, one turquoise and one green seed bead, followed by another bellflower.

THE TURQUOISE SEED BEADS PROVIDE SUBTLE HIGHLIGHTS IN THE TUBULAR NETTING AND ARE ECHOED IN THE COLOURS OF THE ACCENT BEADS.

step 6
Repeat until you have added eight flowers and groups of seed beads in total. Skipping the last three seed beads added, pass the needle back through all the beads and into the netted tube. Repeat at the other end of the tube. Finish off the loose ends of thread (see Finishing a thread, page 35).

This version of netting stitch (see page 64) uses four sets of three beads to form square shapes instead of diamonds, giving lots of scope for embellishment. Size 8 seed beads have been used here to demonstrate how to work the stitch, but when you are more confident, you might like to try using size 11 beads – they create a great effect.

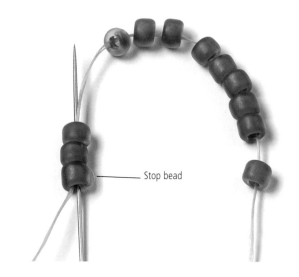

Stop bead

step 2 Thread on another 11 beads, then take the needle through the first set of three beads once more.

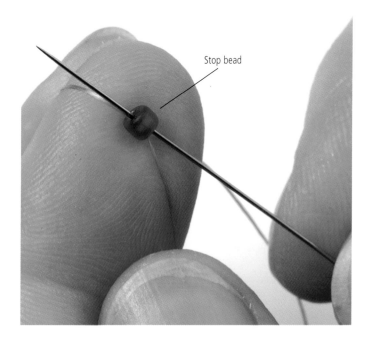

Stop bead

step 1 Thread a beading needle with 1m (1yd) of beading thread and pick up one bead. Slide the bead down to within 15cm (6in) of the tail end of the thread, then bring the needle back up through the bead to create a stop bead.

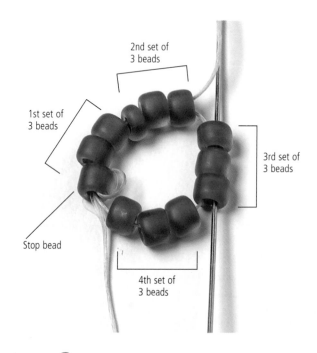

2nd set of 3 beads

1st set of 3 beads

3rd set of 3 beads

Stop bead

4th set of 3 beads

step 3 Thread the needle through the next six seed beads, three beads at a time to keep the square shape of the beadwork. This forms the first square of the net.

BEADER'S TIP

It is important that you always thread the needle through the beads in sets of three beads at a time. This helps to form the square-shaped netting. If you thread through them in one go, you will be encouraging them into a circle shape.

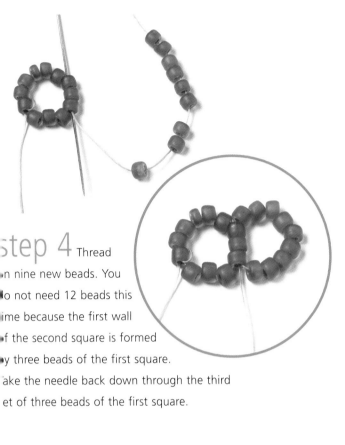

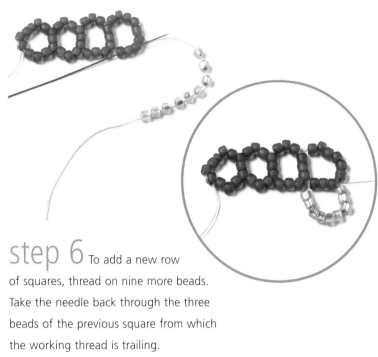

step 4 Thread

on nine new beads. You do not need 12 beads this time because the first wall of the second square is formed by three beads of the first square. Take the needle back down through the third set of three beads of the first square.

step 6 To add a new row

of squares, thread on nine more beads. Take the needle back through the three beads of the previous square from which the working thread is trailing.

step 5 Thread the needle through the next two sets of

three beads of the second square. This brings the needle into the correct position for adding a third square. Continue adding squares until the beadwork reaches the desired length.

step 7 Thread back through

all the beads just added, three at a time. Take the needle through the bottom three beads of the next square along on the original row, so that the needle is in the correct position to add another square. Continue adding new squares and rows in this way until the desired size is achieved.

Project 9: CRYSTAL BRACELET

This is a great little design for showing off some lovely crystal beads, but you could choose another style of accent bead of a similar size if you prefer. The cleverly disguised fastening formed from a beaded loop and fringe adds a simple but effective decorative touch.

MAKING THE NETTING

step 1 Thread 14 seed beads and one crystal onto 1m (1yd) of beading thread, leaving a 15cm (6in) tail end. Pass the needle from the tail end upwards through all the beads once again, then tie a double knot between the crystal and adjacent seed bead. This forms the loop for fastening the bracelet.

step 2 Take the needle back through the crystal, then thread on three sets of three seed beads and one crystal. Thread the needle back through the original crystal to form the first square. This is the same as the square netting stitch described on page 74, but there is a crystal along each side of the square in addition to three seed beads. Take the needle back through the first set of three seed beads and one crystal, then through the next set of three seed beads and one crystal.

Fastening loop · Small link · Crystal square

step 3 Thread on three seed beads, one crystal and three more seed beads. Thread the needle back through the crystal from which the working thread is emerging in the first square. You have now formed the small link that appears between each pair of crystal squares of the bracelet. Take the needle through the first three seed beads and crystal that you just added, so that the needle is in the correct position to add another square.

step 4 Continue adding crystal squares and small links in this way until the required length is achieved. The tassel fastening can be attached to either a crystal square or a small link, so there is no need to worry about whether the correct length is reached at a square or link.

ADDING THE FRINGE

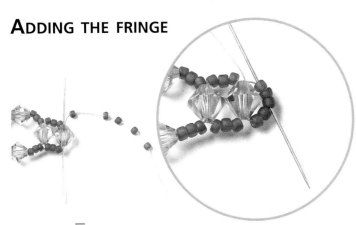

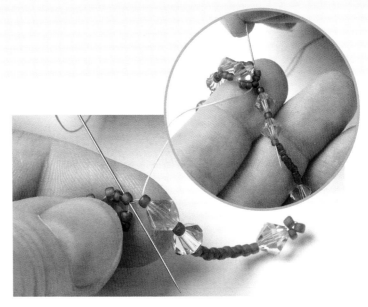

step 5
With the needle coming out of the last crystal, thread on five seed beads. Then pass the needle back through the crystal and the first three of the five seed beads.

1st group of 10 seed beads, where branches will be added later

step 6
Thread on: 1 seed bead, 1 crystal, 1 seed bead, 1 crystal, 10 seed beads, 1 crystal, 3 seed beads. Skipping the last three seed beads, thread the needle back through all the remaining beads just added to form the central fringe (see Adding a fringe, page 102).

step 7
Thread the needle through the middle of the five beads added in step 5. This ensures that the fringe sits centrally on the main netting. Take the needle through the step 5 seed beads and crystal, until it emerges from the middle of the five seed beads once again. Thread down through the central fringe until you are coming out of the first of the group of 10 seed beads added in step 6.

step 8
Thread on eight seed beads to form a second fringe. Skipping the last three beads, pass the needle back up and around as before, until it emerges from the first of the 10 seed beads again, ready to add a third fringe. Make the third fringe using 10 seed beads. Finish off the loose ends of thread (see Finishing a thread, page 35).

PRETTY PURPLE AND LILAC BEADS MAKE THE PERFECT BRACELET FOR A SUMMER OUTFIT, OR YOU COULD TRY BLACK AND GOLD FOR A FORMAL EVENING LOOK.

Project 10: BLUEBELL CHOKER

Czech pressed-glass flower beads in a bluebell design have been used to make this bright and summery choker, but you could easily create an autumnal look by using black or brown cord with accent beads in a leaf design. Rat's tail cord is comfortable to wear and gives an unusual finish.

MAKING THE NETTING

step 1 Using lilac seed beads, work a single line of 29 squares of square netting stitch (see page 74). When finished, tie a double knot between two beads on the last square to hold the beads in place. Do not finish off the ends of thread because these will be used to secure the beadwork to the cord. Fold the line of squares in half to determine where the middle is.

ADDING THE FRINGE

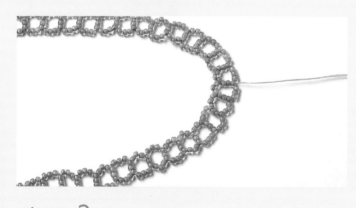

step 2 Join a new thread to the middle of the netting (see Starting a thread, page 34), then thread the needle down through the central row of three vertical lilac beads.

3 sets of 1 blue seed bead and 1 cube bead

1 blue seed bead

1 bluebell

1 blue seed bead

step 3 Add a central fringe (see page 102) by threading on three sets of one blue seed bead and one cube bead. Add another blue seed bead, a bluebell and one more blue seed bead. Skipping the last seed bead added, thread back up through the fringe, the three vertical lilac beads of the netting, then around and down through the next three vertical lilac beads of the netting.

Fringe 3

Fringe 1
(central fringe)

Fringe 2

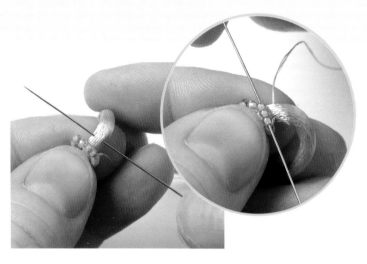

step 4 Add a second fringe in the same way, but with one less seed bead and cube bead at the beginning. Add a third fringe, again using one less seed bead and cube bead at the beginning. Add another two fringes on the other side of the central fringe, staggering the length of the fringes symmetrically. You can either thread through the beads to the other side or pin a fresh piece of thread. Finish off the loose ends of thread in the fringing only (see Finishing a thread, page 35).

step 6 When you are happy with the position, use the threads at each end of the netting to put a couple of securing stitches through the cord. Take the needle through the last three vertical lilac beads of the square netting, then finish off the loose ends of thread as before.

ATTACHING THE CORD AND FASTENER

step 5 Cut a length of rat's tail cord long enough to fit around the neck, adding about cm (2in) at each end for adjustments. Carefully thread the cord in and out of the beadwork squares. Move the beadwork to the centre of the cord with the fringe hanging down.

step 7 Hold the choker up against the neck to check that you are happy with the length. Trim the cord symmetrically if necessary. Attach a flat leather crimp and jump ring to each end of the cord, then attach the lobster clasp to one of the jump rings (see page 119).

CHOOSE YOUR ACCENT BEADS FIRST, THEN COMPLEMENT THEM WITH SEED BEADS AND RAT'S TAIL CORD IN APPROPRIATE COLOURS.

Project 11: BLUEBELL CHARM BRACELET

This is a charm bracelet with a twist. Instead of having traditional charms, pretty Czech pressed-glass flower beads in bluebell and bellflower designs have been used to complement the choker on page 78. These beads give the bracelet a delicate look, but it could be quite dramatic if worked in black and gold for evening wear.

TOOLS AND MATERIALS

- 10g size 11 seed beads: lilac
- 2g size 11 seed beads: blue
- 5g 4mm cube beads: lilac
- 5g 4mm cube beads: blue
- 7–10 bluebell accent beads: blue
- 7–10 bellflower accent beads: amethyst
- Clasp
- Beading thread: ash
- Beading needle
- Beading mat
- Scissors

MAKING THE BEADED BASE

step 1 Using lilac seed beads, work a single row of square netting stitch (see page 74) to fit around the wrist, allowing about 1.5cm (⅝in) for the clasp. The design works best if there is an even number of squares because the cube beads are added to the netting in pairs.

step 2 Add a lilac cube bead inside the first square using a cross stitch. Start by bringing the thread out at the top right corner of the last square worked. Thread on a lilac cube bead, then hold the thread diagonally across to the lower left corner of the netted square.

step 3 Take the needle up through the three vertical seed beads on the left side of the square, then thread the needle back down through the lilac cube bead.

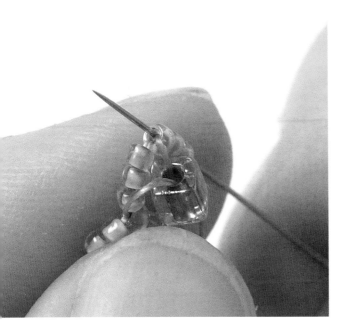

2 lilac seed beads
1 bellflower
1 lilac seed bead

step 5
If you are feeling confident, you can add the fringes of accent beads as you apply the cubes; otherwise, add them at the end. Add each fringe by threading down through the three vertical seed beads on the main netting (see page 102). Position an amethyst bellflower between each pair of lilac cube beads, adding two lilac seed beads, then the bellflower and another lilac seed bead for each one. Remember to skip the last seed bead when threading back up through the fringe into the main netting of the bracelet.

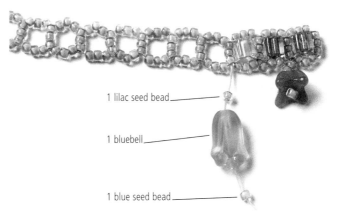

1 lilac seed bead
1 bluebell
1 blue seed bead

step 4
Pass the needle up through the three vertical seed beads on the right side of the netted square. This will straighten the cube within the square, and you will be able to see the cross stitch formed through the cube. Continue adding cube beads in this way, alternating two lilac beads and two blue beads. You will not always be starting from the same position on the squares, but this is not important as long as a cross stitch is formed through each cube.

step 6
Add the bluebell fringes between each pair of blue cube beads by threading on one lilac seed bead, one bluebell and then one blue seed bead. Skipping the blue seed bead, thread back up through the fringe and into the netting as before. Finish off the loose ends of thread (see Finishing a thread, page 35) and attach a clasp (see page 98).

THE DIFFERENT LENGTHS OF THE ACCENT BEADS CREATE A STAGGERED LOWER EDGE ON THE BRACELET, ENHANCING THE FEELING OF MOVEMENT IN THE BEADWORK.

Technique: LOOMWORK

Loomwork has a long-established history, dating back to the first Native Americans and many African nations. The technique is still very much alive today and, as well as being popular with adults, loomwork is a great way to introduce children to beadwork. When you look at a section of loomwork and square stitch (see page 52), it is difficult to tell which is which because the thread pattern is similar. Square stitch does not grow as fast as loomwork, but with loomwork you have the time-consuming task of weaving in the loose ends of thread to secure them.

Creating a design

You can either design freehand directly onto the loom as you bead, or prepare a design on graph paper using coloured pencils. Cross-stitch embroidery patterns are great for translating into a loomed piece of beadwork because they are also designed on a grid system.

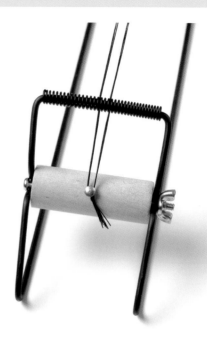

step 2 Turn the spools at each end of the loom so that the pegs face outwards from the loom. Place the knots around the pegs with the threads separated into two halves. If you are weaving a piece that is longer than your loom, wind the extra length of threads around the spool farthest away from you.

THREADING A LOOM

Decide on your bead design. If you are working freehand, you need to decide how many beads wide the design will be so that you can set up the loom accordingly. Use a strong synthetic thread for loomwork.

step 1 Cut one more warp (lengthways) thread than the number of beads wide that the design will be. This design is 9 beads wide, so 10 pieces of thread are required. Cut the thread to the required length, adding a 15cm (6in) at each end for finishing off the threads. Knot the threads together at both ends using a double knot.

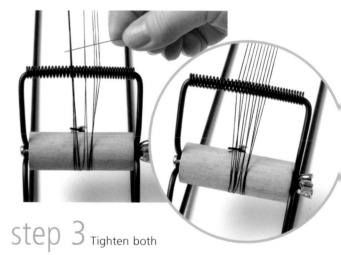

step 3 Tighten both spools until the threads becomes taut over the separator bars. Use a beading needle to lift the threads into separate adjacent grooves on the separator bars. You may need to loosen the threads a little by adjusting the spools while doing this, but remember to tighten them again afterwards.

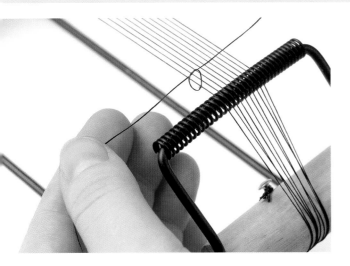

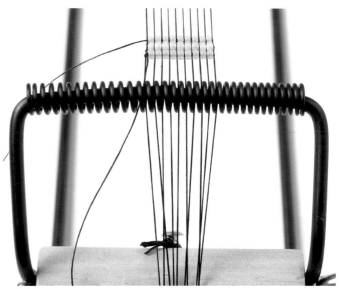

step 4 Once the 10 warp threads are positioned, you need to attach the first weft (crosswise) thread in preparation for adding the beads. Thread a beading needle with 1m (1yd) of beading thread. Tie one end of the thread around the first warp thread in a double knot, leaving a 15cm (6in) tail end.

step 6 Continue adding rows of beads in this way, changing colour and building the design as you go. If you are following a chart, check carefully that you are adding the right colour beads in the correct order to complete the design.

WEAVING THE BEADS

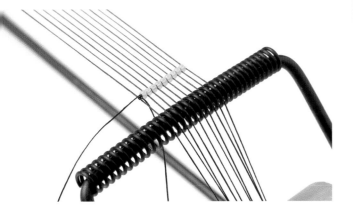

step 5 Thread the first row of beads onto the needle (in this case, nine beads). Position the beads under the loom, pressing them up between the warp threads. Pass the needle and weaving thread through all nine beads, making sure that the needle glides under the warp threads. Holding the beads in place with your finger, bring the needle back through the beads, but this time make sure that it travels over the top of the warp threads. This completes the first row.

FINISHING OFF

- Whenever you finish a length of weaving thread, simply knot a new length of thread onto the outermost warp thread. Remember to leave a tail of thread to allow you to weave in the ends neatly when you have finished beading. When the beadwork has reached the required length, loosen the spools at both ends of the loom and lift the work off.

- Finish off the weft threads by weaving each thread through one or two rows of beads. You can place a double knot between any two beads as you would normally do when finishing off a thread (see page 35), but you need to be very neat or the knot will show and spoil the fabric-like effect that loomwork produces.

- To finish off the warp threads, cut off the knots that you used to secure the threads to the loom; in this demonstration, there would be 10 loose warp threads at each end of the work. Depending on the fastening method you have chosen for the finished item, you may need to work some or all of the warp threads, one at a time, back into the loomwork.

Project 12: FRIENDSHIP BRACELET

This project is a great way to discover loomwork. It is worked from a graph, with pretty little flower motifs set into a pearlized background. The ends are shaped into a point to give a delicate finish. They are worked in square stitch, but as loomwork and square stitch are so similar, the join is almost impossible to see.

TOOLS AND MATERIALS

- 10g size 11 seed beads: cream
- 10g size 11 seed beads: pink
- 5g size 11 seed beads: purple
- 5g size 11 seed beads: green
- Lobster clasp and split ring
- Beading thread: white
- Beading needle
- Small beading loom
- Beading mat
- Scissors

MAKING THE BASE

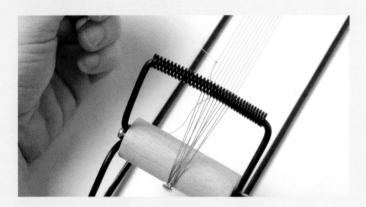

step 1 Thread the loom with 10 strands of beading thread, then add the first weft thread (see Threading a loom, page 82).

step 2 Starting at the top left corner of the chart (see page 85), thread the first nine cream seed beads onto the weaving thread to form the first row of the bracelet. Push the beads up through the warp threads with your finger and pull the needle through the beads beneath the warp threads (see Weaving the beads, page 83).

step 3 Carefully pass the needle back through all the seed beads, making sure you carry the weaving thread over the warp threads this time.

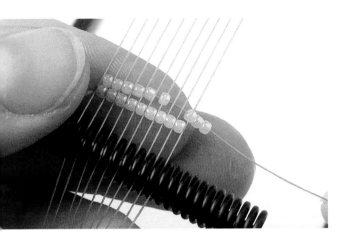

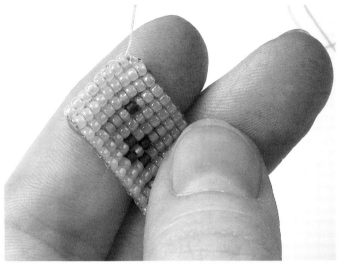

SHAPING THE ENDS

step 4 Thread on all the beads required for the second row and weave them onto the loom as before. Continue in this way, checking carefully that you are following the correct colour sequence on the chart. Calculate the length of loomwork required, allowing for four rows of square stitch to be added at each end, plus about 1.5cm (⅝in) for the clasp. Work the chart design until the required length is achieved, finishing with two rows of cream seed beads to match the first end of the bracelet.

step 5 On the final loomwork row, take the weaving thread back through the final row of beads in the usual way, but bring the needle out of the next to last bead. Remove the beading from the loom.

BEADER'S TIP

This type of loom will only accommodate about 15cm (6in) of beading comfortably, so adding the square stitch ends achieves two things. First, it gives a neat finish; and second, if you need to lengthen the bracelet, you can add several more rows of square stitch the same width as the loomwork section of the bracelet before reducing down to a point. Remember to allow about 1.5cm (⅝in) for the clasp.

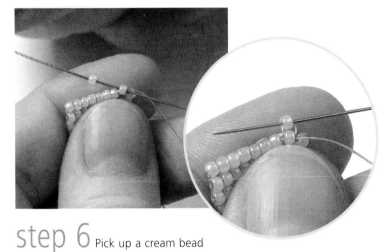

step 6 Pick up a cream bead and pass the needle back through the next to last bead on the final loomwork row. Turn the needle and take it back through the bead just added.

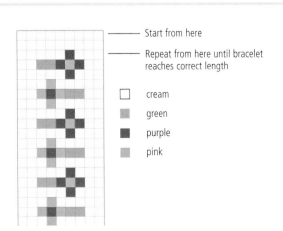

—— Start from here

—— Repeat from here until bracelet reaches correct length

☐ cream

▨ green

■ purple

▨ pink

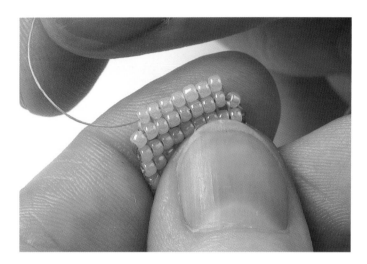

ADDING THE PICOT EDGE

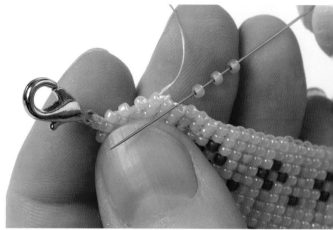

step 7 Continue working square stitch (see Working square stitch, page 52) until you reach the last bead on the opposite side of the bracelet. Do not add a bead at this end so that the width of the bracelet begins to decrease symmetrically.

step 9 Bring the needle up through the last bead when the bracelet is at its full width. Thread on three pink seed bead then pass the needle under the second loop of thread on the edge of the beadwork (see Picot edging on page 104, but note that this picot is being worked in a slightly different way).

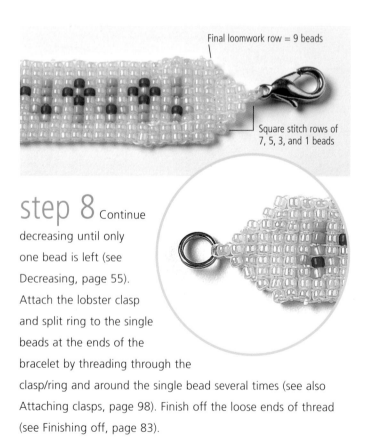

Final loomwork row = 9 beads

Square stitch rows of 7, 5, 3, and 1 beads

step 8 Continue decreasing until only one bead is left (see Decreasing, page 55). Attach the lobster clasp and split ring to the single beads at the ends of the bracelet by threading through the clasp/ring and around the single bead several times (see also Attaching clasps, page 98). Finish off the loose ends of thread (see Finishing off, page 83).

step 10 Bring the needle back up through the third picot bead just added.

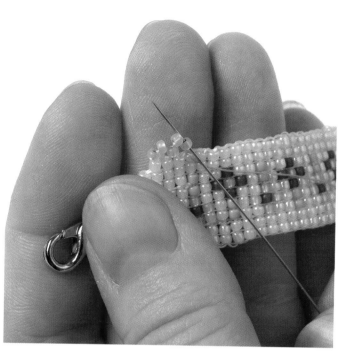

step 11
Thread on two more pink seed beads and take the needle under the next loop of thread along the edge of the loomwork.

step 12
Bring the needle up through the second picot bead just added. Continue along the row in this way until the edge is complete. Repeat on the opposite side of the bracelet.

PRETTY PASTEL FLOWER MOTIFS ARE PERFECT FOR THIS FRIENDSHIP BRACELET, BUT YOU COULD CREATE A DIFFERENT DESIGN IF YOU PREFER. WHY NOT TRY A ZIGZAG DESIGN IN BRIGHT JAZZY COLOURS, OR EXPERIMENT WITH AZTEC PATTERNS IN TERRACOTTAS AND BLUES?

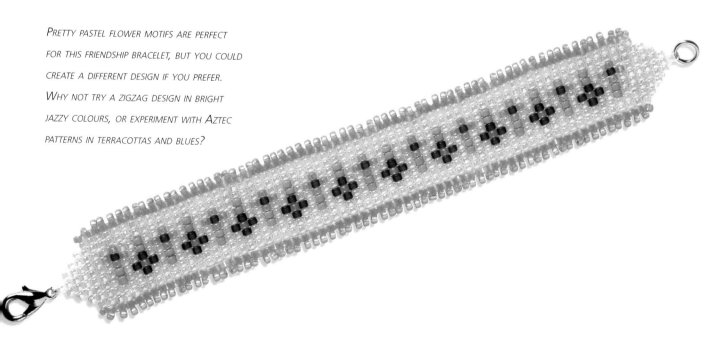

Project 13: SCALLOPED CHOKER

This project shows how versatile loomwork is, achieving the scalloped shape with just a few simple changes to thread tension and bead size. A slightly larger, longer loom than the one featured previously is used for this project. It works the same way but requires a slightly different setup.

MAKING THE CHOKER

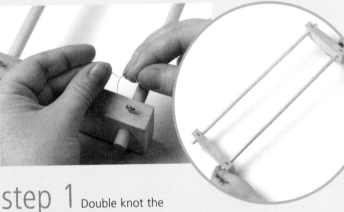

step 1 Double knot the beading thread onto one of the feet of the loom, then pass the thread along the underside of the loom.

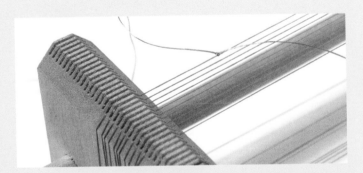

step 2 Take the thread around to the top of the loom and place it in one of the separator grooves. This design requires 11 warp threads because the choker is 10 beads wide. Continue to wrap the warp threads around the loom until you have 11 warp threads in position directly next to one another. Tie the tail end of the thread to the nearest foot on the loom. Tie on a weft thread (see Threading a loom, page 82).

step 3 Thread on 10 light pink seed beads, push them up between the warp threads with your finger and pull the needle through under the warp threads. Take the needle back through the beads, this time above the warp threads (see Weaving the beads, page 83).

step 4 Add a row of lilac, medium pink and then purple seed beads.

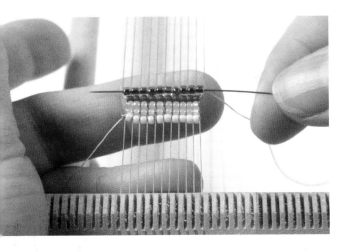

step 6 Work a row of purple, medium pink and then lilac seed beads. Pull the weaving thread slightly to tighten the tension and shape the necklace when working these three rows.

step 5 Add three rows of triangle beads. These will seem far too big and will take a bit of persuading to fit between the warp threads, but persevere. When passing the needle back through them, try to ease them into a curve as you work. This helps them to sit well.

step 8 Shape the ends of the choker to a point and add the clasp in the same way as for the Friendship bracelet (see page 85). Finish off the loose ends of thread (see Finishing off, page 83).

step 7 Work three rows of light pink seed beads, then repeat the sequence from the first row of lilac seed beads. Continue until the choker reaches the required length, remembering to allow for the clasp you have chosen and four rows of square stitch at each end. Make sure that you finish so that the design is symmetrical; you can adjust the number of rows of square stitch at each end, if necessary, to reach the required length (see Beader's tip, page 85). Remove the beadwork from the loom.

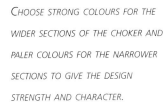

CHOOSE STRONG COLOURS FOR THE WIDER SECTIONS OF THE CHOKER AND PALER COLOURS FOR THE NARROWER SECTIONS TO GIVE THE DESIGN STRENGTH AND CHARACTER.

Herringbone stitch creates a wonderful chevron pattern when worked in both flat and tubular versions. Try experimenting with different shaped beads to create a variety of looks and textures. Herringbone stitch is usually worked with one strand of thread, but use two strands if you require a firm tension for items such as three-dimensional pieces.

Getting the tension right

It can take a while to master the tension of this stitch because the beads tend to move around. This is due mainly to the fact that the pairs you create on the row you are working are not actually linked together until the next row is added. If the tension is too loose, the beads will flop about, making it difficult to see where to make your next move. If the tension is too tight, the beads will buckle up and you will not achieve a chevron pattern. Practice makes perfect, so don't be put off – the results are well worth the effort.

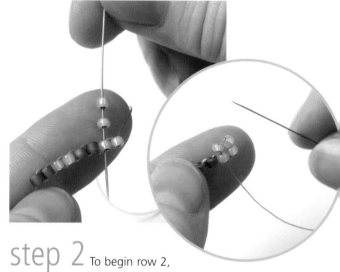

step 2 To begin row 2, pick up a pair of seed beads in the first colour to match the pair of beads at the end of the ladder. Pass the needle down through the second bead on the ladder and gently pat the two new beads so that they sit side by side with the holes facing upwards.

STARTING THE BEADWORK

There are several ways to begin herringbone stitch, but a basic ladder is by far the easiest for a beginner.

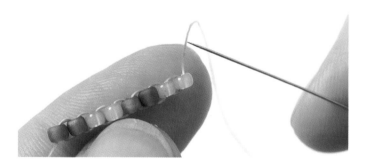

step 1 Make a ladder foundation in the same way as when starting brick stitch (see page 42). Eight beads will make a good-sized practice piece. Use pairs of beads in alternating colours to make it easy to see the emerging pattern.

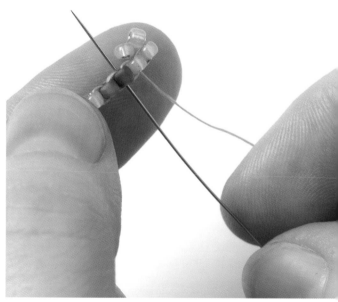

step 3 Bring the needle up through the third bead on the ladder row.

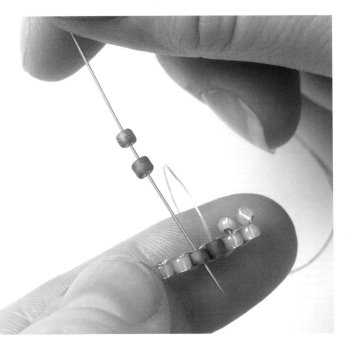

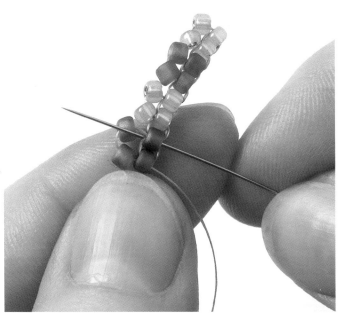

step 4 Thread on the next pair of beads, remembering to change colour to match the pair below on the ladder row. Pass the needle down through the fourth bead along the ladder row. Pat the new pair of beads until they sit side by side with holes facing upwards.

step 6 The working thread is now trailing from the first bead on the original ladder row, so you need to step up to the correct position to work another row. Start by taking the needle up through the second bead on the original ladder.

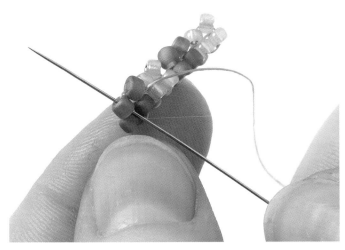

step 5 Continue adding pairs of beads along the row in this way. When the new row is complete, you will notice the herringbone or chevron effect starting to appear, with each pair of beads tilting slightly towards each other. At this point, the beads are sitting in matching pairs. The next row will connect the pairs together.

step 7 Now take the needle across and up through the first bead of the first pair on row 2.

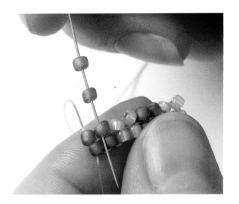

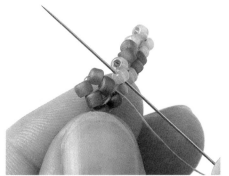

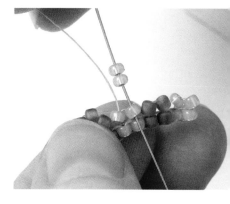

step 8 For row 3, thread on a pair of beads, then pass the needle down through the second bead on row 2.

step 9 Come up through the first bead of the next pair on row 2. This creates a linking stitch between each pair of beads on row 2.

step 10 Thread on two beads in the appropriate colour and bring the needle down through the second bead of the pair below on row 2.

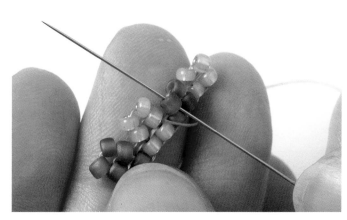

step 11 Pass the needle up through the first bead of the next pair on row 2. Continue adding pairs of beads along the row.

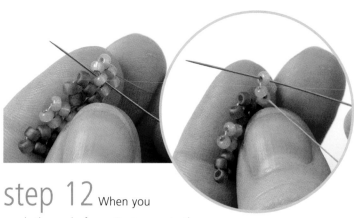

step 12 When you reach the end of row 3, step up to the correct position for row 4 by taking the needle back up through the second bead on row 2, then through the first bead of the first pair on row 3. You are now ready to begin row 4.

step 13 Continue adding rows in this way. As the beadwork grows, a wonderful chevron pattern emerges.

TUBULAR HERRINGBONE STITCH

Of all the beadworking techniques, this stitch produces one of the most attractive tubes, particularly when worked with triangle beads. The following steps are worked in two contrasting colours to enable you to see the rows clearly. Tubular herringbone stitch does slip and slide about at the start, but with a little perseverance you will create a great finished piece.

step 3 To step up to the correct position for row 3, thread up through the next bead on the ladder row, then up through the first bead of the first pair on row 2.

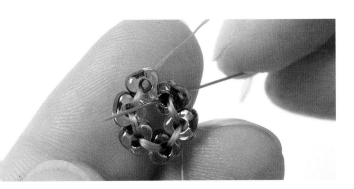

step 1 Make a foundation ladder row (see page 42) using six beads. Form a circle with the holes of the beads facing upwards, then join the beads together by threading through the first and last beads on the ladder several times, ending with the thread emerging from the first bead.

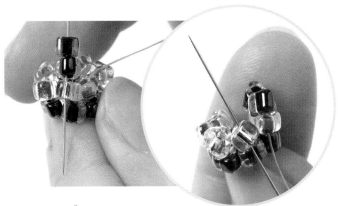

step 4 Pick up two beads and pass the needle down through the second bead of the first pair on row 2. Pass the needle up through the first bead of the next pair. This is the linking stitch.

step 5 Continue adding rows of tubular herringbone stitch until you reach the required length.

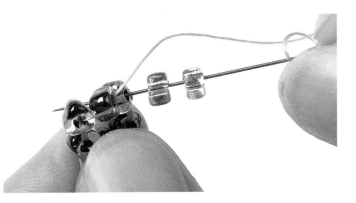

step 2 Thread on two beads in a contrasting colour. Pass the needle down through the next bead on the ladder row, then thread up through the third bead on the ladder. Repeat to add two more pairs of beads.

Project 14: METEOR SHOWER BRACELET

This is a great project to start your journey into herringbone stitch. The flat herringbone base has a lighter stripe running through the centre to provide the perfect base for sparkling crystal accent beads. A classic bar clasp gives this cuff bracelet a classy finish.

MAKING THE BASE

4 black seed beads   2 white seed beads   4 black seed beads

step 1 Using four black, two white and four black size 8 seed beads, make a ladder foundation row (see page 42).

step 2 Work a length of herringbone stitch (see page 90) to fit around the wrist, allowing about 1.5cm (⅝in) for the clasp.

- 15g size 8 seed beads: black
- 10g size 8 seed beads: white
- 5g size 15 seed beads: black
- Selection of accent beads, such as small drop beads, stars and 4mm crystals (one accent bead for every line of herringbone worked for the base)
- Four-bar clasp
- Beading thread: black
- Beading needle
- Beading mat
- Scissors

step 3 When you reach the other end of the bracelet, sew the pairs of beads into a ladder to match the start of the bracelet and to make attaching the clasp easier. Do this by passing the needle up and down through and between the pairs of beads in order to mirror the first end of the bracelet.

ADDING THE EMBELLISHMENT

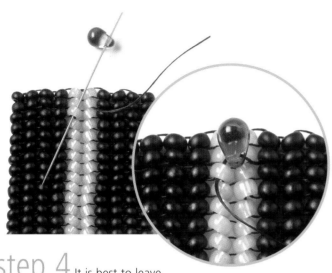

step 4 It is best to leave
the first two rows of white beads at both ends of the bracelet
free from accent beads, which could interfere with the clasp.
Thread the needle down through the first two white beads on
the right-hand side at either end of the bracelet. Thread on a
drop bead, then pass the needle through the third white bead
on the left-hand side. This will make the drop bead sit between
the second and third pair of white beads in from the end of
the bracelet base.

step 5 Continue adding accent beads between the
rows of white seed beads. When attaching the crystals and star
beads, you will need to thread on the crystal or star and then
one size 15 black seed bead. Then, skipping the last seed bead,
thread the needle back through the crystal or star and into the
left-hand white bead on the bracelet base. The seed bead is
there to stop the accent bead from falling off the bracelet.

step 6 Attach the clasp to the ends of the bracelet (see
Bar clasps, page 100). Finish off the loose ends of thread (see
Finishing a thread, page 35).

*SOME OF THE ACCENT BEADS HAVE
A SUBTLE IRIDESCENT FINISH TO ADD
AN EXTRA TOUCH OF SPARKLE TO
THIS SHIMMERING BRACELET.*

Project 15: TUBULAR BRACELET

This design brings the traditional beaded bracelet up to date, creating a bangle effect. When you are wearing the bracelet, the light will catch the sides of the triangle beads beautifully. The finishing touch is the magnetic clasp surrounded by brick stitch, making the clasp look neat and tidy.

MAKING THE TUBE

step 1 Starting with either colour of the triangle beads, make a ladder foundation row using six beads (see page 42). Join together into a circle with the bead holes all facing upwards, then work a rope of tubular herringbone stitch (see page 93), alternating the colours of each row.

step 2 Continue until the bracelet has reached the required length, allowing about 1.5cm (⅝in) for the clasp. When you have added the final row of beads, join the pairs of triangles together by threading up and down through and between the pairs to match the ladder at the start of the bracelet.

ATTACHING THE CLASP

step 3 Bring the needle through any of the end triangles, then thread one section of the clasp onto the needle. Pass the needle down through a triangle on the opposite side of the triangle circle.

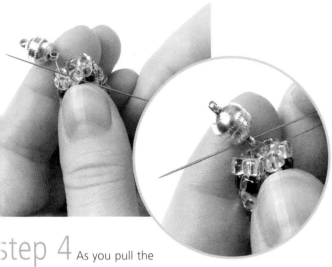

step 6 Pass the
needle back up through
the first seed bead,
then down through the
second seed bead, under
the loop of thread, then
back up through the
second seed bead.

step 4 As you pull the
thread through, centre the clasp over the hole of the tube. Bring
the needle up through the triangle next to the one you came
down through. Thread the needle through the clasp once again,
then back down through a triangle on the opposite side. Repeat
this several times until the clasp feels secure.

step 7 Now work brick stitch in the usual way, adding
one seed bead at a time (see page 42). When you have beaded
around to the start, take the needle back down through the first
seed bead added, then up through the last bead added once
again to secure. If needed, add a second row to cover the
fixing point of the clasp. Repeat at the other end of
the bracelet. Finish off the loose ends of
thread (see Finishing a thread,
page 35).

step 5 To add the wall of brick stitch around the base of
the clasp, start by bringing the thread out of any of the triangles
at the end of the bracelet. Pick up two seed beads, then pass the
needle under the next loop of thread joining a pair of triangles.

*A MONOCHROME
COLOUR SCHEME IS
IDEAL FOR THIS BRACELET,
ALLOWING THE CHEVRON
STITCH PATTERN TO BECOME THE
FOCAL POINT OF THE DESIGN.*

Technique: ATTACHING CLASPS

Choosing an appropriate clasp can mean the success or failure of a finished piece of jewellery, so always buy the best clasp you can afford. Cheap clasps often tarnish or break easily, while more expensive clasps stand out from the crowd and really crown a piece. Learning how to attach a clasp in the correct manner is also important. It is worth taking your time and doing the job well.

SIMPLE CLASPS

Simple clasps, such as this inexpensive but highly decorative example, typically have one small fixing point at both sides. Adding a stem of a few small seed beads at each end of the beadwork will make the clasp easier to open and close.

step 3 Tie a single knot between two beads at this point to allow you to turn the needle and thread it back up through the beads to the clasp.

Smaller beads
for flexible stem

step 1 Thread on three or four small seed beads at the end of the piece of beadwork where you want to attach the clasp. Thread the needle through the fixing point at one end of the clasp.

step 2 Thread the needle back through about five or six beads.

step 4 Thread the needle through the clasp fixing point once again to give added strength. Repeat this journey once or twice until the clasp feels secure. Attach the other end of the beadwork to the other end of the clasp in the same way, remembering to add three or four small seed beads before the clasp. Finish off the loose ends of thread (see Finishing a thread, page 35).

TOGGLE CLASPS

A toggle clasp consists of a ring and a T-bar with a looped fixing point on each one. Always remember to add a stem of a few small seed beads at each end of the beadwork to make it easier to pass the T-bar through the ring.

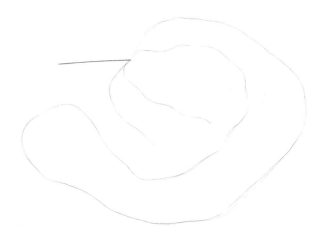

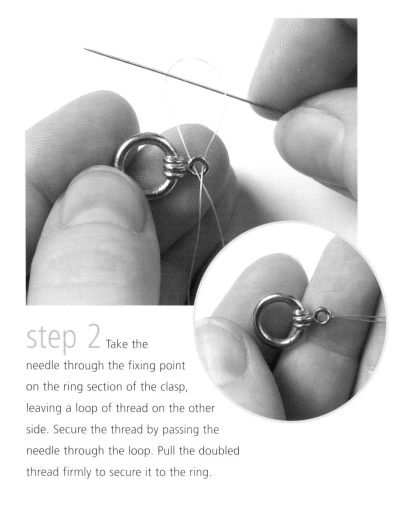

step 1
Using doubled thread will make it easier to attach the clasp and give the beadwork added strength. Pass both ends of a 1.5m (5ft) length of thread through the eye of the needle.

step 2
Take the needle through the fixing point on the ring section of the clasp, leaving a loop of thread on the other side. Secure the thread by passing the needle through the loop. Pull the doubled thread firmly to secure it to the ring.

Smaller beads for flexible stem

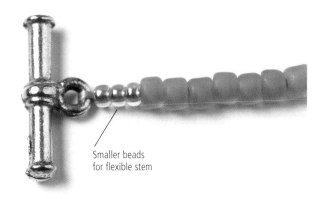

Smaller beads for flexible stem

step 3
Thread on three or four small seed beads, then add enough beads to the core of the piece until you reach the required length.

step 4
Thread on another three or four small seed beads at the other end of the piece, attaching the T-bar section of the clasp in the same way as the ring section. Finish off the loose ends of thread (see Finishing a thread, page 35).

Bar clasps

These clasps are great for cuff bracelets and choker necklaces, because they are long and thin and keep wider sections of beadwork flat and in place. There is a wonderful array of bar clasps available, from plain and serviceable to more elaborate and ornate.

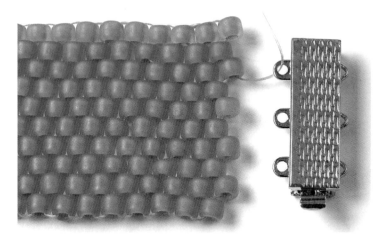

step 1 Place the bar clasp alongside the finished edge of the beadwork, aligning the beads to the clasp fixing points. Bring the needle out through one of the beads nearest to one of the fixing points on the clasp. Pass the needle through the corresponding fixing point on the clasp.

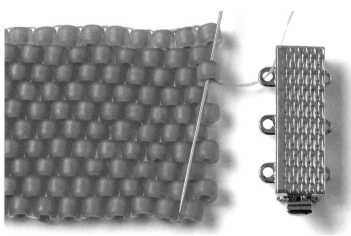

step 2 Thread the needle back through the bead in the main body of the beadwork. Repeat once or twice more until it feels secure.

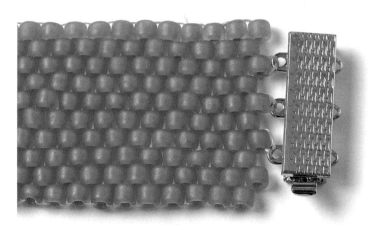

step 3 Repeat in the same way for the other fixing points on the clasp. Attach the other side of the clasp to the other end of the beadwork in the same way.

BEAD AND LOOP FASTENERS

Bead and loop fasteners are a very popular way of finishing off pieces of jewellery. They are one of the most discrete clasps because they can be constructed from the same beads used in the necklace or bracelet, making them an integral part of the piece.

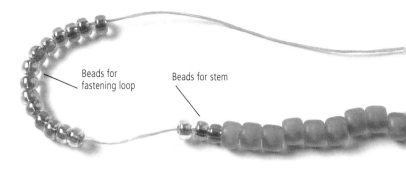

Beads for fastening loop

Beads for stem

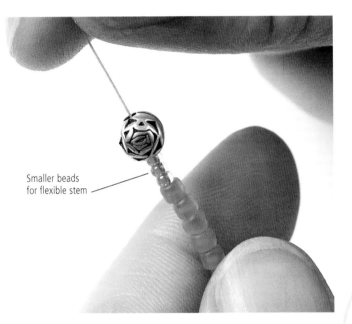

Smaller beads for flexible stem

step 3 Add a stem of three or four small seed beads at the other end of the beadwork. Thread on more beads to make a loop large enough to slip over the bead fastener.

step 1 Using a colour that matches or complements the main beadwork, thread on three or four small seed beads to form a stem for the fastener bead. Thread on the fastener bead and push it down towards the small seed beads.

step 4 Pass the needle back down through the stem beads and into the main body of the work. Tie a single knot between two beads at this point to allow you to turn the needle and thread it back up through the stem and loop beads two or three more times for added security. Finish off the loose ends of thread (see Finishing a thread, page 35).

step 2 Thread on another small seed bead, then take the needle back down through the fastener bead, the three small seed beads and into the main body of the beadwork. Tie a single knot between two beads at this point to allow you to turn the needle and thread it back up through the beads and around the fastener bead two or three more times until it feels secure.

Technique: DECORATIVE FINISHES

There are plenty of patterns, kits and books available featuring wonderful beadwork designs. Here are a few decorative finishing techniques you can use to customize those designs. Never be afraid to add something extra – it could make your beadwork stand out from the crowd.

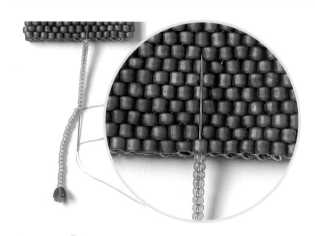

ADDING A FRINGE

Beads drape beautifully when strung as a fringe and look great on almost any beaded piece. You can also create patterns within the fringe to extend the design from the main beadwork into it. Decide whether you want the fringe to be straight or worked into a central point. If the latter, it is best to place the central fringe first and then work outwards, first to one side and then the other. If you work from one end to the other, by the time you reach the centre you may find that the central fringe is too long.

step 2 Skipping the last bead added, thread the needle back through the accent bead and then through all the remaining beads on the fringe. Pass the needle back up through the bead you initially emerged from in the main body of the beadwork.

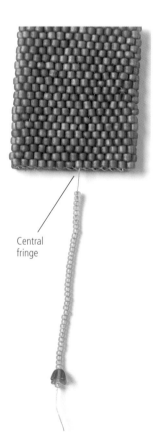

Central fringe

step 1 The best way to centre a fringe is to fold the piece in half and place a needle through the central bead. Attach a new 1.5m (5ft) length of beading thread near to where the first fringe is to be placed. Weave the needle up and down the beads until the thread is coming out of the bead that will hold the fringe. Thread on the required number of beads, in this instance seed beads, and slide them down towards the main beadwork. Add an accent bead if required, followed by an extra seed bead.

step 3 Thread the needle down through the next bead, ready to add the second strand of fringing. Add all the remaining fringes in the same way.

BEADER'S TIP

If you are planning to add a pattern to the fringe, figure out the design on graph paper first using coloured pencils. As you add each fringe, hold the work up to check that the pattern is correct and that each strand is hanging in the right position. If the fringe is too loose, the beads will not sit snugly. If the fringe is too tight, the beads will buckle and the fringe will not drape well.

BRANCH FRINGING

Branch fringing is a great way of adding colour, shape and texture to a piece. This can be achieved by using different sizes of beads together with dynamic accent beads.

Position of
1st side
branch

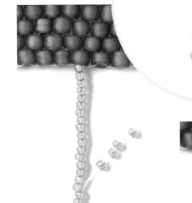

step 2 Thread
on the required number of beads for the branch. Skipping the last bead added, thread back up through the beads of the branch.

Position of
2nd side
branch

step 3 Pass the
needle back into the main strand of fringing and take it through the beads to the place where you wish to add the second side branch.

step 1 Add the first strand of
fringing in the usual way. Skipping the last bead added, pass the needle back up through the beads, with the needle emerging where you wish to position the first side branch.

step 4 Add as many
side branches as you wish, then take the needle back up through the remaining beads on the central fringe and up through two or three beads on the main piece of beadwork. Turn the needle and bring it back down through the beadwork to the position where you want to place the next fringe.

Picot edging

Picot edging is great fun to do and can be added to almost
anything. Several different effects can be achieved, depending
on how many beads are used for each picot and where they
are placed. If three beads are used, they will gather into little
points and look very effective when the central bead is a
different colour to accentuate the point. If more beads are
used for the picots, they look like little frills. Picots can be
added to necklaces, bracelets, earrings and amulet purses –
the possibilities are endless.

step 2 Thread on three beads.

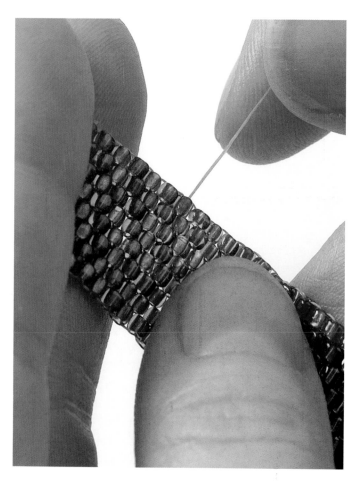

step 1 Bring the needle out of the main body of the
beadwork at the point where you wish to add a picot.

step 3 Pass the needle down through the next bead
along on the main beadwork.

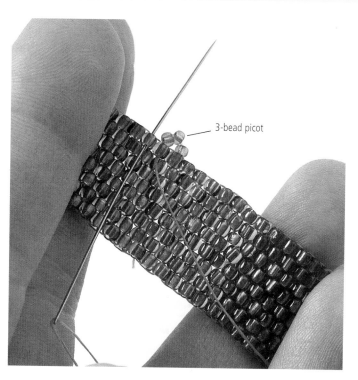

3-bead picot

step 4
Thread the needle up through the next bead along on the main beadwork, making sure that the first picot is pulled up to the beadwork.

step 5
Thread on three more beads to create the next picot. Continue adding as many picots as required.

5-bead picot

step 6
Here, five beads are added to create a different effect – a frill rather than a point.

BEADED LOOPS

Beaded loops are another great decorative addition to any beadwork project. Simple and fairly quick to do, they give instant impact to any piece.

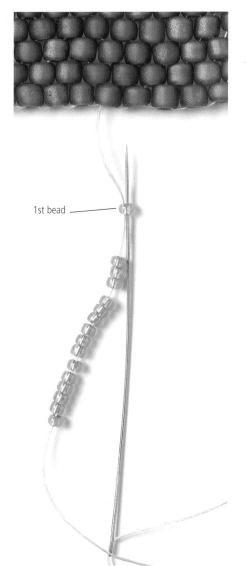

1st bead

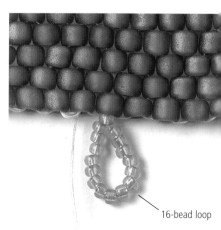

16-bead loop

step 2 Pull the thread through the first bead to form a loop.

step 3 Take the needle back up into the main body of the beadwork. Turn the needle and bring it back down through the beadwork to the position where you want to place the next beaded loop.

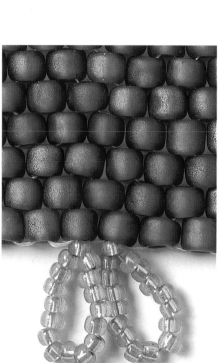

step 4 Keep adding bead loops where required until the design is complete. Remember to pull each loop up every time a new loop is formed or you risk finding unsightly loose threads when the design is finished.

step 1 Bring the needle out of the main piece of beadwork at the place where you wish to position a beaded loop. Thread on the number of beads for the size of loop you require, then pass the needle back through the first bead added.

STRUNG LOOPS

This is another simple but effective way of creating a decorative edge, using strings of beads to form shallow loops. In this example, strings of 10 size 11 beads are looped at intervals of 4 beads along the main piece of beadwork.

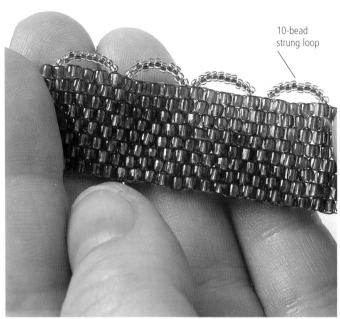

10-bead strung loop

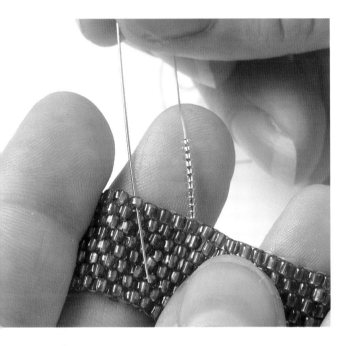

step 3 Continue adding strings of beads along the row until complete, leaving three beads between each string.

step 1 Bring the needle out through the main piece of beadwork where you wish to add a string of beads. Thread on 10 beads, then count along 3 beads on the edge of the beadwork, taking the needle down through the 4th bead.

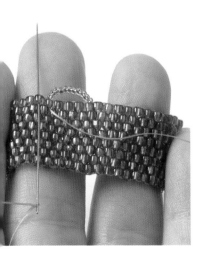

step 2 Pass the needle up through the fifth bead, ready to add the next loop.

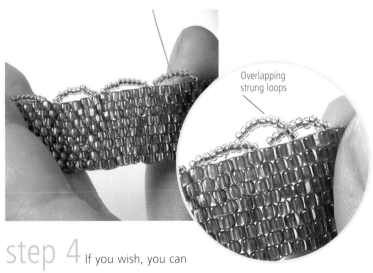

Overlapping strung loops

step 4 If you wish, you can make a return journey along the edge, placing a string of beads between each of the initial loops added. Start by bringing the needle up through the central bead of the three beads missed between the ends of the first loop. Thread on 10 beads and make another strung loop. Continue all along the edge.

Once you enter the world of wire jewellery, the possibilities are endless. So much of the fashion jewellery available today is created using wire as its base. When first using this technique, it is best to choose a very simple project to help build your confidence. The wirework earrings and bracelet on pages 110 and 112 are both suitable for learning basic wirework skills. There are many different tools and materials available for wirework, from wire jigs to coiling gizmos, but only a few items are essential.

Wire

The choice of wire is endless. Most inexpensive wire is plated, which means that the base metal is usually nickel, copper or aluminium, with a coating to give it the same look as precious metal. Also available are many coloured wires. These are coated with either enamel or nylon, and are great for fashion work. However, over long periods of time the colour will wear off. When you first start to work with wire, use manageable lengths of no more than 30cm (12in). This will stop the wire from kinking and looking worn.

Metal chains

Chains are available in both precious and plated metals. They form an ideal base for necklaces and bracelets, allowing you to attach your favourite beads to them using pieces of wire, jump rings or headpins. When choosing a chain, you will need to match the size of the links to the gauge of the wire you will be using with them. Also think about your budget, since chains can be expensive.

WIRE SIZES

When you first go to purchase wire, it can be very confusing. Some companies label their wire in gauges, while others use millimetres. Use the conversion chart below to help when you are selecting wire to buy.

Millimetres	Gauge size
0.2mm	32
0.3mm	28
0.4mm	26
0.5mm	24
0.6mm	22
0.8mm	20
1.0mm	18
1.3mm	16
1.6mm	14

Wire This is now available in many fabulous colours, widths and configurations.

Metal chains Chains are available in many different shapes and sizes, ranging from precious metals to inexpensive craft chains.

ssential pliers

When choosing pliers, buy the best you can afford.
It is a good idea to keep your tools in a case away
from dampness, which may cause them to go rusty.

Flush cutters These do exactly
as they their name implies –
they cut wire, leaving a clean,
wedge-shaped end. They have
a small point, enabling you to
reach into tight spaces – a must
for the wireworker.

Round nose pliers These are
the most important pliers for wirework,
and are used to create all the loops.

Chain nose pliers These
are used for opening and
closing small chain links, hence
their name. They have no teeth, so they will not mark
or make any unwanted impressions in your work.

BEADER'S TIP

If you are just starting wirework, it is a good idea not to spend
too much on your first few reels of wire. You then will not feel
quite so bad when discarding sections of wire that have not gone
exactly to plan. Wirework is all about practice. The more you
handle the wire and tools, the better you will become. Don't
strive for perfection in your early pieces – it is the overall look
that matters. It is a good idea to practise bending and twisting
the wire into loops, wrapped loops and S-bends. You will notice
that the wire becomes smoother and less kinked as you get
used to working with it.

Holding pliers

Position the pliers in the palm of your hand, with one side of the
pliers running alongside the ball of your thumb, and the other
side of the pliers running along the length of your fingers.

Project 16: BEAD-AND-WIRE EARRINGS

A great introduction to working with beads and wire is to make drop earrings using ready-made components such as headpins and earring posts. This project is ideal for using up leftover beads from larger projects. They also make great gifts for family and friends.

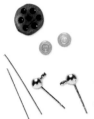

MAKING THE EARRINGS

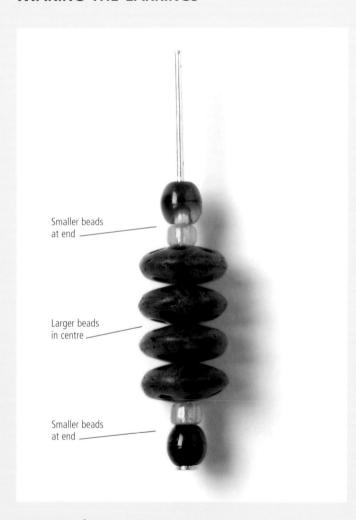

Smaller beads at end

Larger beads in centre

Smaller beads at end

step 1 Thread the beads in the required order onto the headpins. If you are incorporating one or more larger beads into the design, it is a good idea to flank them on both sides with smaller beads. This gives a good balance to the design.

step 2 Use cutting pliers to trim off the excess wire, making sure that you leave about 1cm (⅜in) of spare wire to finish off the earring. If you are new to working with wire, it is a good idea to leave slightly more than you need. Remember that you can always cut off a little more later if you need to.

step 3 Hold the bead drop between your thumb and fingertips. Position the round nose pliers slightly above where the beads are lying on the wire. Bend the wire towards you.

step 4 Move the pliers to the top of the wire and use their tips to roll the wire around to form a loop. If you find that the loop is too large, unroll the loop slightly, cut off another section of wire and then re-roll the loop.

step 5 If the loop looks a little messy, reinsert the pliers and use them to shape the loop more neatly, using a smooth rolling action.

YOU CAN USE ANY COMBINATION OF BEADS YOU LIKE TO CREATE DROP EARRINGS, FROM A SINGLE LARGE BEAD TO THE MULTIPLE BEAD DESIGN SHOWN HERE.

step 6 When you are happy with the loop, use the round nose piers to reopen the loop enough to slip on the earring post. Reclose the loop using the pliers as before. Make a matching earring in the same way.

Project 17: WIREWORK CHARM BRACELET

This bracelet proves that you do not have to spend a fortune to create the latest fashionable look. It is the clever use of colour, shape and texture that gives the bracelet its impact.

MAKING THE BRACELET

step 1 Using cutting pliers, cut a length of chain for the bracelet, allowing about 1.5cm (⅝in) for the clasp.

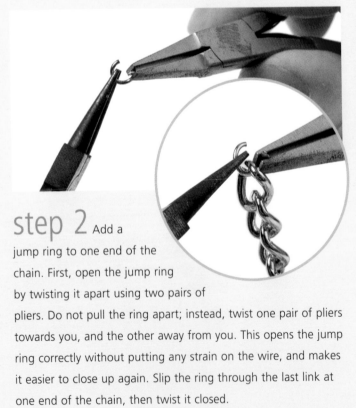

step 2 Add a jump ring to one end of the chain. First, open the jump ring by twisting it apart using two pairs of pliers. Do not pull the ring apart; instead, twist one pair of pliers towards you, and the other away from you. This opens the jump ring correctly without putting any strain on the wire, and makes it easier to close up again. Slip the ring through the last link at one end of the chain, then twist it closed.

step 3 Open a second jump ring and slip it through the last link at the other end of the chain. Slip the lobster clasp onto the ring as well, and then twist the ring closed.

MBELLISHING THE BRACELET

step 4 Add the charms first, spacing them evenly along ne bracelet. Do this using jump rings in the same way as you ttached the lobster clasp.

step 6 Continue adding bead-and-wire drops in this way until you are happy with the finished result. It is worth making a few different drops and experimenting with them, fixing them to the bracelet to see how they look. Remember that they are relatively easy to remove and reposition.

tep 5 Now add the bead-and-wire drops by threading eads onto gold headpins and then looping the end of each in around a link in the bracelet chain (see Bead-and-wire arrings, page 110).

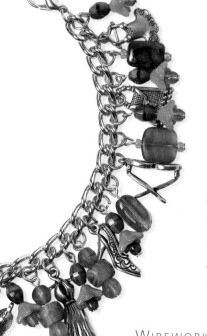

THE GOLD CHARMS AND CHAIN COMPLEMENT EACH OTHER, WHILE THE BEADS ADD COLOUR TO THE DESIGN. BRIGHT RED ACCENT BEADS ADD VIBRANCY TO THE COLOUR SCHEME.

Project 18: RETRO FLOWER BROOCH

This retro-inspired brooch can be completed relatively quickly and is great fun to make. Wiring accent beads and seed bead leaves onto a sieve brooch base is really easy to do.

MAKING THE PETALS

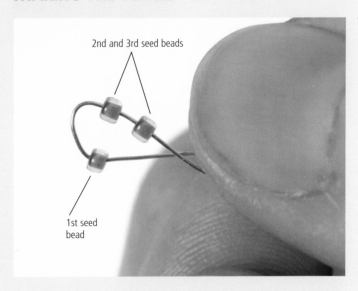

2nd and 3rd seed beads

1st seed bead

step 1 Use cutting pliers, cut a 30cm (12in) length of beading wire. Make a bright pink petal by threading three seed beads onto the wire. Bend the wire in half and position the first seed bead to one side of the bend and the other two beads to the other side.

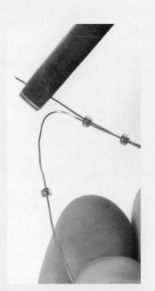

step 2 Pass the end of the wire where the first bead is sitting through the other two beads to form a loop. Use flat nose pliers to pull the wire all the way through until the beads sit close together in a triangular formation.

step 3 Thread three more beads onto either end of the wire. Push them up next to the first three beads and bend the wire around so that the three beads just added sit neatly underneath the two above. Pass the other end of the wire through the beads just added, so that there are two ends of wire running through them.

step 4 Continue adding rows of beads in this way, increasing one bead each time. When you have reached eight beads in width, decrease one bead each time until you are down to two beads. This is the end of the petal that will be attached to the brooch base.

Work 2 of these

Work 2 of these

Work 8 of these

step 5 Work a second bright pink petal with a central row of eight beads, eight pale pink petals with a central row of seven beads, and two burgundy petals with a central row of eight beads.

WIRING THE ACCENT BEADS

step 6 Cut several 10cm (4in) lengths of beading wire. The leaves used here have horizontal (top-drilled) holes, so the wire is threaded through the holes. Cross the two ends and twist them around each other once. If your flowers have vertical (centre-drilled) holes like those used here, thread one end of wire up through the flower halfway, add any colour seed bead and then thread the other end of the wire up through the flower. Twist the wire to hold it in place as before. The number of accent beads you need will depend on the size of the sieve brooch.

ASSEMBLING THE BROOCH

step 7 Attach the seed bead petals by passing the wire down through the front of the sieve section of the brooch in the second row of holes from the outer edge. Twist the wires around each other on the back of the sieve to secure the petal in place. Flatten the wire down and trim the ends to about 2.5cm (1in).

step 8 Continue to attach the petals in a pleasing design. Attach the accent beads to the centre of the sieve in the same way, making sure that you cover any gaps. Attach the sieve section to the brooch back by clamping the holding bars into place using flat nose pliers.

THE DIFFERENT TONES OF COLOUR IN THE FLOWER BEADS ARE ECHOED IN THE BEADED PETALS TO CREATE A HARMONIOUS DESIGN.

Technique: STRINGING

Sometimes when you find some beautiful beads, all you need to do is thread them together in a string to create a truly unfussy look that will display the beads to their best potential. You can string the beads on a variety of different materials, including beading wire, memory wire, suede, leather and ribbon. The only real skill required is to learn how to finish the ends of the threading material.

SIMPLE STRINGING

This is a quick and easy way of creating a bracelet or necklace using plastic-coated beading wire with knot cups and a clasp.

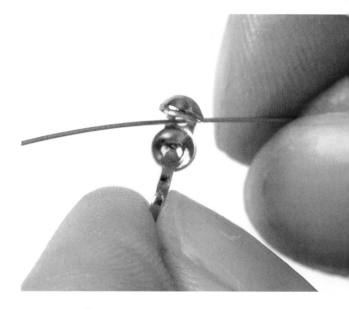

step 2 Pass one end of the wire through the hinge of the knot cup.

step 1 Lay out your chosen beads and try several different arrangements until you are happy with the look. Cut the required length of plastic-coated beading wire, allowing an extra 15cm (6in) for the knot cups and clasp. Thread the beads onto the wire.

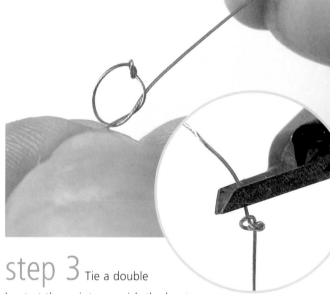

step 3 Tie a double knot at the point you wish the knot cup to sit, remembering to leave enough wire on the other side to finish. Using cutting pliers, trim the wire close to the double knot, then put a dab of clear nail polish over the knot.

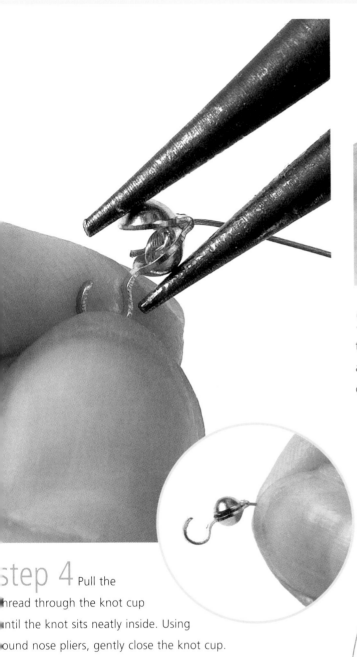

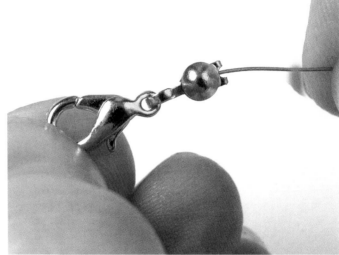

step 5 Slip a lobster clasp onto the open loop of
the knot cup. Using round nose pliers, close the loop. Repeat
at the other end of the wire, adding a knot cup and a jump ring
or split ring.

step 4 Pull the
thread through the knot cup
until the knot sits neatly inside. Using
round nose pliers, gently close the knot cup.

*SIMPLY STRINGING BEADS ONTO WIRE IS A GREAT
WAY TO DISPLAY BEADS TO THEIR BEST EFFECT.
CHOOSE WITH A SIMPLE CLASP RATHER THAN A
MORE ELABORATE ONE SO THAT YOU DO NOT
DETRACT ANY ATTENTION AWAY FROM THE BEADS.*

USING MEMORY WIRE

If you want to create almost instant chokers and bracelets, memory wire is the medium to work with. The wire remains in a coil even after beads have been added, hence its name. It is tough and durable, and a great way to introduce children to beading. Use strong wire cutters to cut the required amount of memory wire. Never use a delicate pair because they will be ruined by the wire.

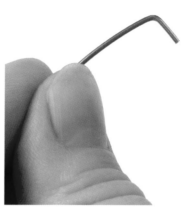

step 2 Bend the wire downwards, then bend the wire back on itself to form a loop.

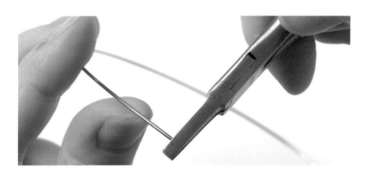

step 1 Place one end of the memory wire between the jaws of a pair of flat nose pliers.

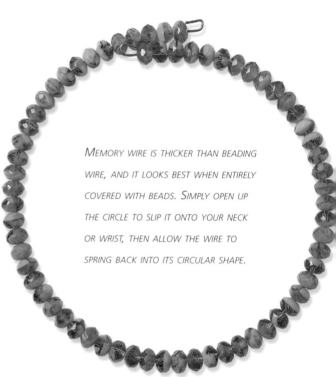

MEMORY WIRE IS THICKER THAN BEADING WIRE, AND IT LOOKS BEST WHEN ENTIRELY COVERED WITH BEADS. SIMPLY OPEN UP THE CIRCLE TO SLIP IT ONTO YOUR NECK OR WRIST, THEN ALLOW THE WIRE TO SPRING BACK INTO ITS CIRCULAR SHAPE.

step 3 Using the unbent end of the memory wire as a needle, thread on the beads until only about 6mm (¼in) of wire is unbeaded. Bend this end of the wire over to form a loop, as before, to finish the piece.

BEADER'S TIP

Add a central pendant to memory wire chokers by hanging the pendant from a jump ring at the centre of the beaded wire. Instead of finishing the ends by bending the wire to form a loop that will stop the beads from escaping, as shown here, you can buy half-drilled beads to glue onto the ends of the wire.

USING FLAT LEATHER CRIMPS

Large beads can be threaded onto suede, leather or ribbon. These necklaces or chokers can simply be tied at the back of the neck, but a more professional look can be obtained with the use of flat leather crimps on each end of the material. When these are secured, attach a lobster clasp and jump ring to the ends of the flat leather crimps.

step 2 Using round nose pliers, bend one side of the crimp over. Reposition the pliers to bend the other side over so that it sits on top of the first side, trapping the material inside.

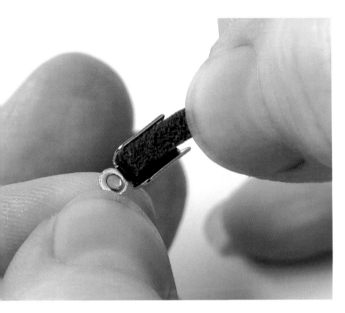

step 1 Place the cord into the flat leather crimp so that the end of the cord aligns with the end of the crimp.

step 3 Open a jump ring using two pairs of pliers, such as round nose and flat nose pliers (see page 112). Slide the jump ring through the loop of the crimp. Slip a lobster clasp onto the jump ring, then use the pliers to close the jump ring. Add a jump ring to the other flat leather crimp to complete the fastening.

You do not have to be an accomplished knitter to create bead-and-wire jewellery. Only basic knitting skills are required, all of which are explained here. As a general rule, 0.2 or 0.3mm wire is the easiest to knit with. Work a small section to test if the wire is suitable for knitting. If it is too fine, the wire will snap; if it is too thick, it will be almost impossible to knit with. Bamboo needles are best because the wire does not slip about quite as much as when worked on aluminium needles. The size of needles you use really depends on the effect you want to achieve, but 2–2.75mm needles are good for working with 0.2mm wire, and 4mm needles for 0.3mm wire. You could use bamboo skewers if you do not have any needles.

Getting the tension right

The tension (usually referred to as gauge in knitting) has to be correct from the start because it is difficult to adjust afterwards. You need to keep the wire quite loopy on the needles to enable you to form stitches easily. Work a test piece to see whether you need to adjust your tension before knitting the main piece.

step 1 Thread about 10g of beads directly onto the spool of beading wire without cutting it. Keep pushing the beads down towards the spool end of the wire.

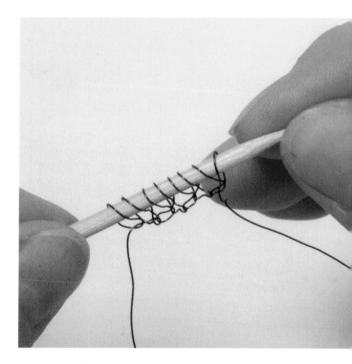

step 2 Cast on the number of stitches required for your design (see box, opposite, for a simple cast-on technique). As a rough guide, eight stitches will produce a 5cm (2in) wide section of knitting.

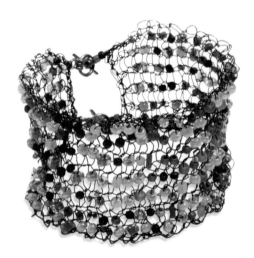

WIRE KNITTING LOOKS VERY MESSY TO START WITH, BUT KEEP GOING AND YOU WILL SOON SEE GREAT RESULTS. THIS BRACELET HAS BEEN FINISHED WITH A PAIR OF TOGGLE CLASPS (SEE PAGE 107).

KNITTING SKILLS: CASTING ON

Casting on is the process of making your first row of stitches on the knitting needle. There are several different ways of casting on; the thumb method shown here is the simplest.

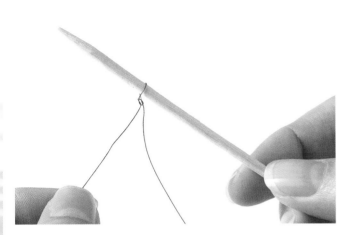

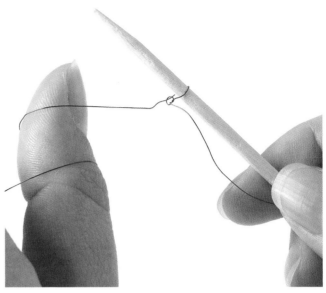

step A Wrap one end of the wire around the needle and make a slip knot, leaving a 15cm (6in) tail of wire. This forms the first stitch.

step B Hold the needle in one hand and grip the working end of the wire with the fingers of your other hand. Wrap the wire around your thumb to form a loop.

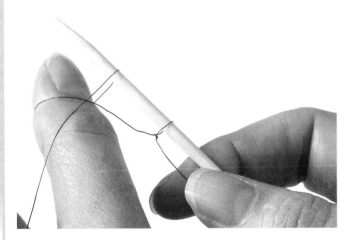

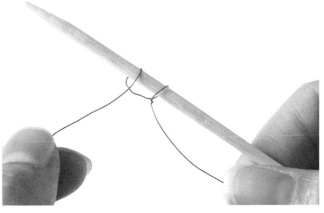

step C Push the tip of the needle up through the loop on your thumb.

step D Slip your thumb out of the loop and gently pull the working end of the wire to tighten the new stitch on the needle, remembering to keep it fairly loopy. Repeat this process to cast on as many stitches as required.

step 3 Knit three rows (see box, right) without any beads.

step 4 Knit the first stitch of row 4 in the usual way, then push several beads up into the palm of the hand holding the working end of the wire. Remember to keep the tension of the wire loose.

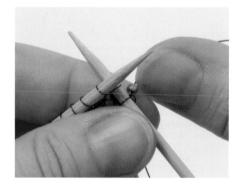

step 5 As you are about to knit the second stitch, push a bead up behind the crossed needles, ready to be knit into the wire. Knit the second stitch in the usual way.

KNITTING SKILLS: KNIT STITCH

The knit stitch is the most basic stitch used to make a knit fabric and is very easy to master. Hold the needle with the cast-on stitches in your left hand and the empty needle in your right hand.

step A Insert the right needle into the centre of the first stitch from front to back so that the two needles cross each other with the right needle behind. Make sure that the working end of the wire is behind the needles.

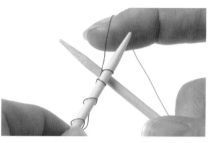

step B Using an index finger, wrap the working end of the wire anticlockwise around the tip of the right needle.

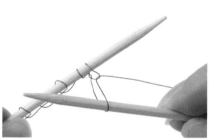

step C Use the right needle to pull the wrapped wire through the stitch on the left needle to create a new stitch on the right needle.

step D Slip the original stitch off the left needle, then continue knitting along the row in this way.

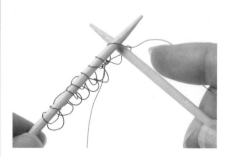

step E Swap the needles at the end of each row so that you begin the new row holding the needle with the stitches in your left hand and the empty needle in your right hand.

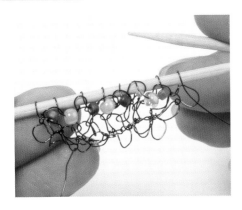

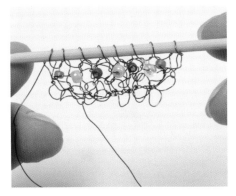

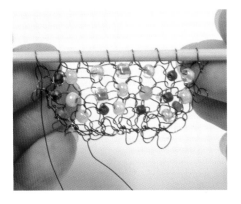

step 6
Continue along the row, knitting a bead into each stitch until you reach the final stitch. Knit this stitch without a bead. If you included a bead in the end stitches, they would stick out through the side of the work.

step 7
Work a row without adding any beads. This does two things – it makes the beads go farther and gives you a flat side that will sit comfortably against the skin.

step 8
Continue alternating beaded and unbeaded rows until the required length is reached. Work three unbeaded rows to match the first end of the knitting, then cast off (see box, below). Finish off the wire ends by winding the wire around itself to secure, making sure there are no sharp edges.

KNITTING SKILLS: CASTING OFF
When you have finished the knitting, you need to cast off to make a neat edge that does not unravel.

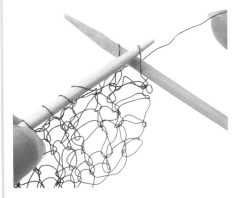

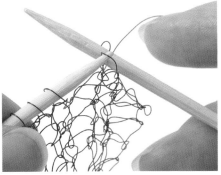

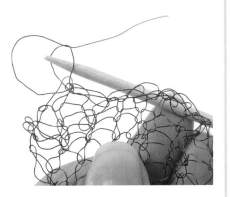

step A
Knit the first two stitches in the usual way. Insert the tip of the left needle into the first of these knit stitches.

step B
Lift this stitch over the second stitch and slip it off the right needle so that you have only one stitch on the right needle. Knit the next stitch on the left needle so that there are two stitches on the right needle once again. Lift the first of these stitches over the second stitch and slip it off the right needle as before.

step C
Continue casting off stitches in this way until the end of the row. Cut off the wire, leaving a 15cm (6in) tail. Thread the tail through the last stitch, remove the needle, and tighten.

RESOURCES

Societies and Groups

Contact your local library for details of bead societies, guilds, and craft groups in your area. Alternatively, a quick internet search will produce a list.

UK

**The Bead Society of
Great Britain (BSGB)**

1 Casburn Lane

Burwell

Cambridgeshire CB5 0ED

www.beadsociety.freeserve.co.uk

The Bead Study Trust

2 Frank Dixon Way

London SE21 7BB

www.beadstudytrust.org.uk

The Beadworkers Guild

PO Box 24922

London SE23 3WS

0870 200 1250

www.beadworkersguild.org.uk

Crafts Council

44A Pentonville Road

London N1 9BY

020 7278 7700

www.craftscouncil.org.uk

Glass Beadmakers UK

GBUK Middle House

34 Grecian Street

Aylesbury

Buckinghamshire HP20 1LT

www.gbuk.org

AUSTRALIA

The Bead Society of Victoria

PO Box 382

Abbotsford

VIC 3067

http://home.vicnet.net.au/~beadsocv

Craft Australia

Level 1, Suite 7,
National Press Club

16 National Circuit

Barton

ACT 2600

craft@craftaustralia.com.au

www.craftaus.com.au

Craft South

PO Box 8067

Station Arcade

SA 5000

craftsouth@craftsouth.org.au

www.craftsouth.org.au

NEW ZEALAND

Creative New Zealand

info@creativenz.govt.nz

www.creativenz.govt.nz

**New Zealand
Polymer Clay Guild**

8 Cherry Place

Casebrook

Christchurch 8005

sales@polymerclay.co.nz

www.zigzag.co.nz

Suppliers

UK

The Bead Merchant

PO Box 5025

Coggeshall

Essex CO6 1HW

01376 563 567

www.beadmerchant.co.uk

The Bead Shop

21a Tower Street

Covent Garden

London WC2H 9NS

020 7240 0931

www.beadshop.co.uk

Beads Unlimited

PO Box 1

Hove

Sussex BN3 3SG

01273 740 777

www.beadsunlimited.co.uk

Beadworks

16 Redbridge Enterprise Centre

Thompson Close

Ilford, Essex 1G1 1TY

020 8553 3240

www.beadworks.co.uk

Brighton Bead Shop

21 Sydney Street

Brighton

Sussex BN1 4EN

01273 740 777

www.beadsunlimited.co.uk

Creative Beadcraft

20 Beak Street

London W1

020 7629 9964

www.creativebeadcraft.co.uk

Earring Things

Craft Workshops

South Pier Road

Ellesmere Port

Lancashire L65 4FW

www.beadmaster.com

Exchange Findings

11–13 Hatton Wall

London EC1N 8HX

020 7831 7574

GJ Beads

Court Arcade, The Wharf

St Ives, Cornwall TR26 1LG

01736 793 886

www.gjbeads.co.uk

International Craft

Unit 4

The Empire Centre

Imperial Way

Watford WD24 4YH

01923 235 336

www.internationalcraft.com

Kernowcraft

Bolingey

Perranporth

Cornwall TR6 0DH

01872 573 888

www.kernowcraft.com

The London Bead Company

339 Kentish Town Road

London NW5 2TJ

0870 203 2323

Londonbead@pipex.com

www.londonbeadco.co.uk

Polymer Clay Pit

3 Harts Lane

Wortham

Diss

Norfolk IP22 1PQ

01379 890 176

www.polymerclaypit.co.uk

Rashbel Marketing

24–28 Hatton Wall

London EC1N 8JH

020 7831 5646

www.rashbel.com

AUSTRALIA

The Bead Bar

Shop 3, Metcalfe Arcade

80 George Street

The Rocks

NSW 2000

02 9247 5946

www.thebeadbar.com.au

Bead Hive
Shop 42, Citi Centre Building
145 Rundle Mall
Adelaide
SA 5000
08 8223 5773
www.beadhive.com.au

Bead Needs
1/11 Elm Park Drive
Hoppers Crossing
VIC 3029
03 8742 2866
www.beadneeds.com.au

Bead Station
11b Spring Street
Reservoir
VIC 3073
03 9471 1736
www.noimagevision.net.au

The Bead Tree
Fullarton
Adelaide
SA 5034
08 8271 4977
www.thebeadtree.com.au

Bead With Me
Unit 4, Springwood
Professional Centre
18 Dennis Road
Springwood
Brisbane, QLD 4127
07 3208 0068
www.beadwithme.com.au

Bead World
1/7 Villiers Drive
Currumbin
QLD 4220
07 5534 1333
www.beadworld.com.au

Benjamin's Crafts
868 Beaufort Street
Ingelwood, WA 6052
08 9370 2132
www.benjaminscrafts.com.au

Cabeadle
24 Market Plaza
Gouger Street
Adelaide, SA 5000
08 8410 3838
www.cabeadle.com

Craft on the Internet
53a High Street
Taree, NSW 2430
02 6552 4188
www.craft.ontheinternet.com.au

StitchnBead
Launcestone, TAS 7250
03 6344 2717
www.stitchnbead.com.au

NEW ZEALAND
Bead Bazaar
Shop 5b
101 Broadway Avenue
Palmerston North
06 356 8612
www.beadbazaar.co.nz

Beadbox
59 Pitt Street
Auckland
09 309 4440
www.beadbox.co.nz

Bead Gallery
18 Parere Street
Nelson
03 546 7807
www.beads.co.nz

The Bead Hold Ltd
Shop 17, Bishops Gate
Business Centre
Corner Te Irirangi Drive
and Bishop Dunn Place
Botany South
09 274 0324
www.thebeadhold.co.nz

The Bead Shop
66 Stanley Street
Queenstown 9297
03 442 3239
www.beadshopnz.com

Beadz Unlimited
Christchurch Arts Centre
Worcester Boulevard
Christchurch
03 379 5126
www.beadzunlimited.com

E Beads Direct
PO Box 6477
Dunedin North 9001
02 262 2184
www.ebeadsdirect.com

String of Beads
23 Liardet Street
New Plymouth 4601
06 759 6985

Tiger Eye Beads
2 Manners Street
Wellington
04 384 7761
www.tigereyebeads.com

Village Beads
148 Jackson Street
Petone, Lower Hutt City 6009
04 566 3240
village.beads@xtra.co.nz

Websites

www.beadandbutton.com

The website for *Bead & Button* magazine.

www.beadcollector.net

Online network of bead collectors dedicated to sharing accurate information about beads.

www.bead-database.org

A global interactive bead database featuring images and information about beads from all over the world.

www.beadexpo.com

An annual conference and bazaar.

www.beadingtimes.com

An online beading magazine.

http://beadwork.about.com

There is an active forum and plenty of links and articles on this site.

http://groups.yahoo.com/group/beadcollectors

Internet forum for those interested in collecting, studying, or working with beads.

http://home.easelsoft.com/archives/beads-l.html

Interactive bead database.

www.interweave.com/bead

The website for *Beadwork* magazine.

www.members.cox.net/sdsantan/beadfairies.html

A useful resources site with lots of links and tips.

www.thebeadmuseum.com

Website for The Bead Museum, with its collection of over 100,000 beads and beaded artefacts.

INDEX

CREDITS

Many thanks to The Bead Scene for supplying all the beads and
equipment used in this book.

The Bead Scene
PO Box 6351
Towcester
Northamptonshire NN12 7YX
+44 (0)1327 811-101
Stephanie@thebeadscene.com
www.thebeadscene.com